How to Live
with a Psychic

How to Live with a Psychic

Your Guide for Maintaining a Happy Relationship when Someone You Love Gets Weird

Crystal Hope Reed

Reed&Carstens
PUBLISHING

HOW TO LIVE WITH A PSYCHIC

Copyright © 2017 by Crystal Hope Reed.

All rights reserved. Printed in the United States of America. No part of this book may be used or reproduced in any manner whatsoever without written permission except in the case of brief quotations embodied in critical articles or reviews.

This book is a work of non-fiction but some names have been changed or omitted for privacy purposes.

DISCLAIMER: The information shared in this book is for personal growth and educational purposes only. Readers are responsible for their own actions and therefore, the author and publisher do hereby disclaim any liability to any party for any loss, damage, or disruption caused by the implementation of techniques suggested herein. Additionally, the healing methods described in this book are not intended as a substitute for the advice of physicians or psychiatrists. Anyone who has a physical health or mental health concern should visit a licensed medical provider.

For information contact:
Reed & Carstens Publishing
2633 Lincoln Blvd. #523
Santa Monica, CA 90405
http://www.CrystalHopeReed.com

Cover design by Brett Carstens
ISBN: 978-1-945031-00-7

First Edition: January 2017

CONTENTS

INTRODUCTION 1
WHO AM I TO TELL YOU WHAT TO DO?............................5
LIFE WITH A PSYCHIC..13
THIS IS A BONDING OPPORTUNITY 21
BUT WHAT IF THEY'RE JUST CRAZY?..............................57
KEEPING THEM ATTACHED TO THIS VERSION OF REALITY..75
GROUNDING AND PROTECTION....................................103
GEARING UP (TOOLS) 119
TAKING CARE OF YOURSELF 127
TYPES OF PSYCHIC ABILITY 151
DON'T JUST TAKE MY WORD FOR IT............................199

INTRODUCTION

So they're psychic. Now what?

Your life used to be relatively normal. You had normal problems with normal solutions. Things weren't always easy but there were resources to consult when an unfamiliar issue arose.

But now your loved one talks to dead people or has disturbing—and accurate—precognitive dreams. Perhaps he or she doesn't leave the house anymore because they're flooded with strangers' emotions while out in public. Sometimes they wake up claiming to have left their body overnight, and you have to admit, they provide details that seem impossible for them to know. Or occasionally, objects "just move" when your significant other is nearby, without a rational explanation.

Welcome to the club.

No matter what flavor of psychic activity is manifesting at your house, you've already learned that you're not just a witness to it. You're a participant in the sense that the change impacts your relationship and the way your partner views the world that you share. And odds are good that you can't talk to your usual stable of advisors about what's going on because not only do they have no experience with anything like this, but you fear they might think you're crazy (or lying, or evil).

That's why, as someone who has already overcome these challenges, I want to assure you: You're not alone, and it's going to be OK.

This isn't how I expected my life to play out either, of course. I grew up thinking psychic ability was nonsense and even when I came around to accepting it as a theoretical possibility, I certainly never imagined it would impact me so profoundly every day.

My "psychic in residence," Brett, has ended up having powerful abilities, but he wasn't always like this. When we first got together, sure, he'd had more paranormal experiences than the average person (or lots of average people combined), but we didn't think of him as "a psychic." In retrospect we realize he'd been dabbling with the psychic realm his whole life, but it wasn't until his abilities manifested in a major way and the house filled up with other-dimensional visitors, almost overnight, that we started experiencing the challenges that often accompany developing psychic ability.

To say it caught us off guard is an understatement. And while it was a huge adjustment for him, there were a ton of books, videos, and support groups for developing psychics so he had access to resources when he wanted them. But what about me? Where was I supposed to learn how to live with a psychic?

I had to make sure our life didn't fall apart. I had to make sure *we* didn't fall apart. I had to battle internally with how this conflicted with my own worldview. Just to name a few things.

I could have read self-help books about the experience from his "person in psychic development" perspective but it wouldn't have helped me figure out how to keep him from making rash, life-changing decisions or telling everyone we know about his "crazy" ideas before we were ready for the consequences. Where were the books to teach me what he would need from me and what I should do while he was going through this metamorphosis? There weren't any.

Fortunately for us, I'm a counselor by both training and nature, which definitely helped. But even with that background I relied heavily on good ol' trial and error to keep us on track.

How to Live with a Psychic is the book I needed back then. It contains practical advice for maintaining (or improving) your relationship through this period of growth. It also covers the foundational information, terminology, and techniques that will allow you to understand what's happening and will prepare you to be an active participant, if you so choose.

Your experience is certainly extraordinary but I meet more and more people all the time who are going through a similar shift. Some couples are weathering the transition without much difficulty, while others, unfortunately, have been pushed to separation or divorce. Your relationship's survival depends on your answer to this one question: Are you going to be torn apart by your circumstances or are you going to proactively use this opportunity to become a stronger team?

This is your guidebook for coming out ahead. My advice, combined with your own instincts, will surely help you take command of your situation. You've survived many challenges in life and this is no different. As always, you just need the right information. And now you've found it.

Chapter 1

WHO AM I TO TELL YOU WHAT TO DO?

When I say I grew up in Santa Monica, California, most people will associate that with affluence. Our city certainly has more than its share of celebrities and wealthy residents now, but the Santa Monica of the '70s and early '80s was actually a very different place. It was a predominantly middle-class city with a small-town beachy feel, combined with many of the trappings of the Los Angeles metropolitan sprawl such as gangs and a significant homeless population.

Ours was a blue-collar household. More importantly, a non-religious household. Not anti-religious, just non-religious. My parents weren't biased against anyone for holding religious beliefs but they were unknowledgeable about and disinterested in world religions, despite the fact that there was fervent religiosity on both sides of the family a few generations back.

These days, most of the major religions of the world are in the forefront of our news and media so we're all more aware than we used to be, but during my childhood the subjects of God, rituals, holy books, and the possibility of souls or an afterlife just never arose in conversation. We weren't avoiding those topics, they just weren't present in our family thought process, even though many people around us were participating in a religious lifestyle of some sort in their own homes. You remember how it was—back before social media made everything we did everybody else's business.

During my enlistment in the Navy in the early '90s I decided I was an atheist. I was utterly clueless about religion and it seemed to me at the time that atheism was the only rational choice presented by the people around me (who I wrongly assumed actually knew what they were talking about since they appeared to know at least a little bit, which was more than I did). According to them, either I was a Christian or I must be an atheist/heathen. Never mind the other major religions like Judaism, Islam, Hinduism, or Buddhism. It was almost like they'd never even heard of those options.

So I decided that since I didn't believe in my fellow sailors' assertion about an old guy sitting on a throne up in the clouds, I must be an atheist. I suffered the wrath of my counterparts almost every day for taking that stand, even though I was never the one to start the conversation because it really didn't matter to me either way. But it really seemed to matter to them.

Everything changed when I returned home after my enlistment. I took a comparative religion class in college and my worldview blew up. Not only was I finally exposed to the philosophies of all the major and minor religions (which explained most of global politics to me, by the way), but I realized that I resonated strongly with the idea of reincarnation. This, of course, was incompatible with atheism and was a subject that had been completely absent from any conversation in my childhood. In retrospect, I give my college-age self a lot of credit for being willing to decisively change course despite the discomfort of having to say, "I've been wrong my whole life."

The crack in the dam

Around that time, *X-Files* was becoming the most popular show on television. I devoured it as weekly diversion but also dared consider, in my newly opened mind, that maybe there really were more truths out there. I sought the company of others who could at least entertain the idea that the Universe contained more than what we had already counted, categorized, and catalogued. (I found my scientist and engineer friends to be the most resistant to these possibilities at the time, which seemed counterintuitive for people who were supposed to be seekers of truth and new information.)

In the late '90s (and my late 20's) I was given the opportunity to be part of a pilot program that was testing out past-life regression (a form of hypnotherapy where you view yourself in a past life in your mind, while still being conscious of what is happening around you now) as an alternative to regular therapy.

The regressionist and I got along famously and had a blast. According to her, I had a greater talent for detail and vividness under hypnosis than almost anyone else she'd met. I felt like I was actually walking around in these historical settings, just with a degree of detachment. Maybe it can be compared to acting. Even when you're highly immersed in your character, you're also still fully yourself, witnessing your own actions and surroundings.

My sessions weren't really focused on therapy but instead on what I later heard referred to as "past-life tourism"—the act of exploring other times and cultures "in person." However, the simple act of viewing one's past life has a way of healing the lingering issues related to that life without having to process them at length, so it's like therapy only without the work.

During my many regressions I saw myself as male, I saw myself as female. I sometimes died tragically, sometimes of natural causes. Never heroically. In a few cases I was even the town drunk or village idiot. During sessions I was able to name and describe places I've never seen and to produce obscure facts that I was able to verify through later research, like laws governing teenage gypsy boys in the mid-18th-century Austro-Hungarian Empire.

The best part was seeing people I know now. Apparently the eyes really are the windows to the soul because even though people looked completely different, when we made eye contact I instantly knew who they were from my current life. I saw friends, old boyfriends, my parents, and even a couple of my former students. It made clearer the idea of having a soul group: souls who reincarnate together to support each other or teach each other lessons in service to our evolution.

My past-life regressions were some of the most fun I'd ever had. I was in my element—my mind—and having incredible adventures. And I had a sort of twisted pride in considering myself (besides the regressionist) the most eccentrically enlightened person I knew.

Until I met Brett.

July of 2001. We fell in love ridiculously fast and were inseparable from day one. We had similar family backgrounds and our moral compasses and interests were almost eerily in sync. And talk about "eccentrically enlightened." I may as well have been in pre-school.

Brett has always been known to his family and friends as a "ghost magnet." He gets approached by strangers and told, "You have little sparkly things floating around your head (or stomach)." One time we had a mouse in our bathtub. Brett grabbed a broomstick and told the mouse, in plain English, "Climb on the stick and I'll put you outside" and sure enough, the mouse wrapped his tiny little arms around the stick and held on so Brett could put him through the open window. I'll spare you all the details, but you get the general idea about the out-of-the-ordinary guy he has always been.

I am inarguably most comfortable in the cerebral realm so for the first several years this was all pretty academic for me. He would report seeing movement and entities that I couldn't see, and though I believed him (and the animals sometimes reacted), to me it was still an abstraction. And it was definitely his thing, not mine.

One time in those early days I was choked by a ghost while trying to fall asleep at a hotel on Fremont Street in Las Vegas. I felt hands touching my neck and was somehow aware of a mass of violently rageful energy hovering over my head and torso. When I turned on the lamp next to the bed, Brett rolled over and said, "What's wrong? You look like you've seen a ghost." And of course he couldn't have been more right.

But despite the fact that incidents like these made the spirit world undeniably real in a personal way for me, the vast majority of the time I still considered it just his thing and we went on about our fairly ordinary lives for the time being.

And then the flood gates opened

Since I had taken a one-day intro course on animal communication (pet psychic) a few years before I met him, I had a cursory understanding of how someone like Brett could operate in more dimensions than the typical person. And yet I still only had an intellectual conceptualization of what he'd been experiencing viscerally his whole life.

But one day several years ago, BAM! The fabric of reality began to tear in a way that was noticeable even to someone like me and intense even for someone like him.

Our house is now often like Grand Central Station—full of entities the average person can't see (but can often feel, even though they don't know what's going on). I remember one time soon after the big shift, the paranormal energy was so palpable that my father told me, "Do your voodoo shit when I'm not here," even though we weren't actually doing anything.

Spirits and other entities seem to be drawn to Brett's brightness in other dimensions, where perhaps most of us are dim, dull, or practically invisible and therefore don't garner their attention. These visitors range from pure manifestations of good, to neutral (human spirits, for example), to embodiments of negativity. (I haven't embraced the concept of evil *per se*, in the way that many people define it, though we've dealt with some really nasty buggers.)

There's stuff that exists that I didn't even believe in until I experienced it firsthand. I'm so thankful that I've honed my own senses over the years so I can corroborate at least a fraction of what he perceives or experiences.

Seeing or hearing spirits and energies that other people can't sense sometimes makes a person feel like they're having a psychotic break. It can cause isolation from loved ones. It can result in shame and self-destructive behavior. This is often due to pressure from various institutions (e.g. the medical/psych profession, some religions, mainstream education) to reject these abilities in ourselves and others. It can really take a toll.

But fortunately, most people who are developing spiritual or psychic abilities will just need support from their loved ones while traversing the rocky patch at the beginning where they feel crazy and alone. Then they'll be able to return to their everyday lives (with a few adjustments that won't necessarily seem like such a big deal once everything is said and done).

I understand, it might all sound absurd—unless you're living it. So that's why I've chosen to write this book—to teach you *How to Live with a Psychic*. (Or medium, healer, empath, etc.)

Since I've already been in some approximation of your shoes, let me help you understand what the psychic in your life is going through and teach you some effective ways to support them. Your own life will be that much better for it.

As with any self-help book, not every piece of advice or every scenario described will apply to every reader. Act on what works for you and just make a mental note of the rest because maybe it will come in handy later. These tools are intended to empower you, not to create a reliance on a "program" or to supplant your personal wisdom. In fact, they are specifically designed to help you maintain dominion over your kingdom, not the other way around.

Chapter 2

LIFE WITH A PSYCHIC

Certainly any particular day with my partner will be vastly different from a day with your partner because that's just human nature. Even when we have a lot in common, we are individuals living unique lives meant only for us. But when it comes to supporting a loved one through difficult phases of psychic development, there is a tremendous amount of commonality so it's valuable to focus on the issue from that perspective.

Common challenges

Here's a list of issues and changes that arise so regularly that they're thought of as universal for new psychics. Maybe you'll recognize some from your current experience.

Increases in sensitivity. Lots of people with emerging psychic abilities develop heightened sensitivity to food, drinks, light, sound, or crowds. Even imagery, or the texture of clothing. Basically, they now are made uncomfortable, either physically or mentally, by things that didn't used to bother them or perhaps they even enjoyed in the past. (We'll talk more about this later but a lot of sensitivities diminish or return to normal states after psychics get their skills under control.)

Related to this are increases in emotional sensitivity and intensity. Your loved one may now be quicker to tears or anger than they were previously. A person who didn't used to experience anxiety may frequently feel that way now. How much of this is based on their own physical and energetic changes and how much is due to them being increasingly reactive to others' emotions would have to be determined on a case-by-case basis, but the functional result is the same: they might be more touchy and moody than before.

Their heightened sensitivity also means they might want to avoid places like hospitals, cemeteries, and even animal shelters, where emotions run high and spirits are likely to be hanging around in greater number.

Changes in sleep pattern. There could be a lot of reasons for this. Maybe they stay awake at night now because they see spirits moving through the house and it fascinates or frightens them. Maybe they need less sleep because they're so highly energized, or they need more sleep because the process of integrating so much new information is exhausting. Some psychics have trouble getting to sleep because they're thinking too much or because they have other-dimensional visitors vying for their attention. Brett and I find that late-night hours are more active so movement, sounds, and physical sensations often keep us up.

Different people go different ways with this, but sleep disruption is almost guaranteed in some form or another. This is an area that could impact you directly on a regular basis if you sleep in the same room with someone with developing abilities.

Illnesses. Some illnesses associated with newly developing psychic ability are stress based, but others are manifestations of changes to a person's energetic body structure or chakras. Or illness could be their Higher Self's way of making sure they slow down for a while because something significant is happening. Headaches, nausea, and other aches and pains are common.

A college classmate of mine fell down in her apartment and couldn't get up for three days because she was in a daze. She lived alone and was terrified. When she was finally able to get up off the floor she had no physical issues but had gained telepathy and the ability to read people's past lives just by looking at them. Though she was able to demonstrate the telepathy convincingly to our class, I wasn't a believer yet so I simply filed away this case in my doubting mind as anomalous and unexplainable.

Most physical reactions won't be so extreme, of course, but I just wanted to give that example of how one's health can be tied intricately to spiritual events with no apparent physical causation or side effects. Sometimes, though, genuine health issues will arise concurrently with spiritual growth issues, so don't neglect to make a doctor's appointment, if concerned.

Redirection of focus and interest. Making the leap from living a typical life to experiencing the realities that are outside of humans' normal perception can be mind blowing. It often results in people reevaluating their priorities or at the very least, devoting a significant amount of their time and brain space to contemplation.

Until it becomes integrated into their life, your partner might seem obsessed with the idea of the paranormal. They might drop some of their typical interests and redirect their mental energy toward study of the esoteric. Depending on their particular skills and how little they feel in control of themselves, they might avoid certain activities out of discomfort or fear that they'll make a scene in public. You have to just respect and tolerate any of their avoidance tendencies at this point.

Don't underestimate the power of the changes that are happening within them. We have a friend who was already psychically skilled but who is currently experiencing a big bump up in his abilities (it just started happening spontaneously one day) and he's having to take a break from work and live off his savings. The shift in his energy is so disorienting that he can't concentrate on work. I'm sure his family is concerned, but this just is part of the cycle for some people. Eventually he will stabilize again and get back into the world.

People with developing skills might also partially reject the trappings of material life and become more drawn to nature.

From experience I can tell you that their intensity of focus is annoying at times and worrisome at others, but it does subside once the novelty wears off, so hang in there.

You may fear that these kinds of changes will make your partner somewhat unrecognizable, but they're still the same person you fell in love with. When Brett reflects on his evolution, he says he just feels like a better, more authentic version of himself, but still himself.

Hopefully this book will alleviate your concerns and help you enjoy participating in your significant other's growth instead of fearing or dreading it.

Unexplainable things start to happen around the house. The psychic person will likely start seeing little movements around the house and depending on your own level of latent psychic ability, you might, too. You know, the flashes of movement you notice in your peripheral vision that you can't see when you turn to look directly. (This happens because paranormal activity takes place primarily in other dimensions and our senses are calibrated to register the wavelengths associated with our typical human experiences. However, our peripheral vision is designed to facilitate low-light vision so it is sometimes able to pick up subtler images, like spirit movement.)

Two possible reasons for seeing more movement—and I'm open to there being others—are 1) that it's always been around and he or she is just starting to notice it, and 2) that due to their increased psychic ability, they are drawing more activity. I would guess it's a combination of both.

Instances of physical items moving when your significant other is around are less frequent but are certainly not out of the realm of possibility of what could be happening.

It's easy to freak out over that phenomenon (which is often called poltergeist activity) because it's outside of what we're taught is normal. But most of the time it's nothing to worry about. It could just be your partner's amped-up energy affecting matter on the physical level. Or maybe it's one of those other-dimensional beings you've noticed lately, trying to get your attention. Both possibilities may seem outrageous but for now just focus on whatever helps you get through the day.

Memories resurface. It's not unusual for people in this growth phase to start remembering incidents from childhood that point to latent psychic ability or earlier brushes with the paranormal.

Is there a family legend about a grandma who used to read tea leaves, or a ghost the whole family saw at Thanksgiving dinner once? Does your husband's mother tell about how, when he was a toddler, he would describe who was going to come to the door right before the doorbell rang? Did your wife used to think she could hear what her pets were saying before she "grew out of it?" How many children do you know who have "invisible friends?"

These are fairly routine stories that we usually stash in the backs of our brains as anomalies until the viability of psychic ability is brought to our present awareness. You may find your partner digging up a bunch of these childhood anecdotes now because they're starting to make sense. This process might manifest as joyful nostalgia or it might trigger an identity crisis. It will depend both on the degree to which it contradicts any rigid worldviews and how traumatic or pleasant the original experiences were.

They start talking to people you can't see. There are a whole range of "people" that psychics can hear/see/sense that a "muggle" can't. (Thank you, J.K. Rowling for such a perfectly useful word.)

Some of these entities are ghosts, which (for the most part) are just humans or animals who haven't moved on to the next phase yet. We don't notice them most of the time because they exist in a dimension that our standard five senses don't register. But your psychic might suddenly become aware of all the spirits hanging around in a space that seems empty to you.

When psychics initially become tuned in to this other dimension, it can be fascinating, scary, or annoying, depending on what's going on. Your significant other may only be able to see or hear them, or they may be contacted directly by the ghosts with pleas for help. Either way, it can be startling and take some getting used to.

Entities that almost all psychics eventually tend to connect with are their Spirit Guides (which are not the same as Angels, by the way, even though many people mistakenly think they are). A Spirit Guide is often a human soul who has evolved to the point that they now stay on "the other side" instead of reincarnating and has volunteered to act as spiritual support for someone who is here on Earth.

I know people like to think that their Spirit Guides are their favorite grandma who passed over and that sort of thing, but that is actually the exception, not the rule. Many of your Guides are with you since birth so there's no way you could have known them in this life. However, it might be someone you knew from many lives ago. Or possibly a soul you've never met incarnated but who sticks with you from life to life.

Your partner might see images of ghosts or Spirit Guides in their mind, or they might see them with their eyes, existing outside of themselves. They might hear messages from either type of spiritual entity in their mind, or they might hear the words like someone is standing close to them and whispering directly into their ear. And while it might make you nervous that they're losing their mind by talking (aloud or in their head) to people you can't see, it's standard operating procedure for people with psychic abilities to be interacting with entities in other dimensions.

This list of challenges is intended to be broad and general, just to reassure you that we have some experiences and concerns in common that I can teach you to overcome. I'll be addressing these topics and many others in detail throughout the book.

Let's now get into the nuts and bolts of how to live with a psychic.

Chapter 3

THIS IS A BONDING OPPORTUNITY

As with other major life changes, such as marriage, the birth of a child, or changing jobs, the emergence of esoteric abilities in a partner is often a make-or-break point in a relationship. And this particular challenge is sometimes even more stressful because there's no readily available source of support. Such situations can test both your personal fortitude and your commitment to each other, have no doubt.

Fortunately, the same basic rule applies to learning to live with a psychic as with any other challenge—*your attitude makes all the difference.* If you decide you're going to be happy today, you most likely will be, barring any extreme unexpected circumstances. And of course the opposite is equally true. Like this famous quote from Henry Ford:

"If you think you can do a thing or think you can't do a thing, you're right."

I hope you find this idea empowering because it's true. And what it means in this context is that you have an opportunity for a stronger relationship and more interesting life than ever before, based largely on your decision to let it be so.

Expect the future to be something better

You're going to hear me talking a lot about intention in relation to many different aspects of living with a psychic. It's important because on some levels, we are all creating through mere thought, whether we're doing it consciously and proactively or not.

The power of intention is the concept behind the popular book you may have heard about: *Creative Visualization*. Or you may remember the 2006 movie called *The Secret* that talked about using "the law of attraction" to improve our lives.

Unfortunately, the movie's assertion that we can manifest trivial things like our ideal parking spot at the mall through positive thinking caused many people to miss or dismiss the overall message: Intention is an extension of our consciousness and carries great weight in how our lives play out on an energetic level.

Or said differently, our thoughts over the long term end up shaping our tangible experience.

It's commonly accepted that having a positive or negative attitude will mostly draw more of the same to us. For people with trauma or tragedy in their lives, this can seem like a condemnation, as if we are blaming them for their own misfortune. Sometimes it is a fair accusation, like in the case of women who think poorly of all men and then somehow only end up dating men who reinforce their bias. But child abuse, the death of family members, etc., are exceptions and of course we wouldn't claim the victim is responsible for drawing that pain to themselves through not being positive enough.

And though karma and the perceived unfairness of life are indeed worthy topics for discussion, let's save them for another time.

For now let's just focus on the fact that having a clear and focused intention for a certain outcome contributes to us getting what we want. The more specific the intention and the stronger we believe in it, the more likely it is to manifest.

I feel fortunate that my master's program embraced not only traditional and cutting-edge counseling techniques and theories, but also the spiritual aspect of our human experience and how it influences our behavior and healing. They emphasized the power of intention as a key in achieving our own goals and also as an important skill to teach our clients.

As part of that training, they taught us to attach the following saying to the end of any prayer, visualization, or request as an indication that we intended to manifest the best outcome possible:

This or something better, for the highest good of all concerned.

So for example, when envisioning a future outcome you might like—such as a bigger house—be as specific as possible in imagining and describing the new place, but also include that phrase at the end.

"I want a six-bedroom, two-story house on two acres with a pool with a waterfall and no neighbors for half a mile on each side. This or something better for the highest good of all concerned."

This add-on is very important because maybe you'll inherit a great house that's the same size as your current one but it will eliminate your mortgage payment. Maybe a bigger house and property would soon become too much to take care of. Perhaps you're going to meet someone really important but only if you stay put. Or what if the move to the bigger house of your dreams would unknowingly deprive one of your children of a major opportunity in the future? There are a lot of potential reasons why it might not be in your best interest to get exactly what you think you want right now.

Just be open to the idea of receiving goodness, and open to the idea that life might still be good even if it's different from what you imagined.

How that translates to this work of strengthening your relationship during a challenging time is keeping yourself open to the possibility that the results will be even better than you possibly think they can be. Don't limit the potential of your future by restricting it to manifesting only in the ways that you are currently able to conceive.

Thank goodness life doesn't just give us what we think we want all the time, right? I mean, would you want to be stuck with the life you assumed you'd have when you were 15? That boy or girl may have had some good ideas but their vision lacked the richness of a full adult life because it was based only on their experience up to that point.

Most of us didn't stick with our first jobs either, and isn't it great that we didn't have to? We grow so much as we learn and have deeper experiences. To be stuck as a former version of ourselves would be so stifling.

As Ray Kroc (you know, the McDonald's guy) asked, "Are you green and growing or ripe and rotting?"

So try to keep a "beginner's mind" as you move forward. (This is the Buddhist concept of setting aside the presumption that we already know how things are. We can learn and experience more when we have an open mind.) Expect that this period of transition will have a positive outcome and don't waste time trying to orchestrate every aspect of your life into a predetermined end product. When has that ever really worked anyway?

Be the person your partner can turn to

Here's the biggest key to success in this scenario: Be the one your partner can turn to. Be the one they can trust. Be the one they know will support them.

If you only took this one piece of advice from this book, you would already have the most important tool you need to make the best of your situation.

People in these circumstances need someone to share the journey with them. If someone you love were experiencing a more commonplace milestone or trauma (e.g. looking for a job after graduating from college or suffering a major illness) it might be easier or more natural to figure out how to support them. You might not even pick up a book about it because you'd already have some point of reference for what to do next.

But in the case of developing psychic abilities, you probably don't have any experience yet and your significant other might sound and feel crazy sometimes, so it can be harder to get your head around what they are experiencing or needing.

However, here is the main point: *If your significant other can't talk to you, if they can't trust you in this moment of vulnerability, be warned that they will find someone else to fill that role.* It's fine if that's an acceptable outcome for you, but if you want to maintain your position at the hub of their operations, you will need to demonstrate that they can trust and talk to you about this, no matter what.

They will indeed benefit from talking to others eventually, but you won't need to be jealous of that if you've established yourself as their primary emotional support by being willing and available to hear what they're going through, even when you'd rather not.

Initiate the conversation

The truth is that none of the psychic modalities are a problem in themselves; the fear, confusion, and self-doubt that often accompany psychic development are the problem.

Therefore, the most important thing you can do to manage this situation and allay your partner's discomfort is to ask what's going on so they don't feel like they're in it alone.

This advice is so simple and obvious that perhaps it doesn't seem to warrant mentioning, but when a situation is overwhelming or uncomfortable we sometimes ignore it and hope it goes away instead of facing it. Don't do that. It will only make circumstances worse.

Most story plots have at the root of their conflict miscommunication or lack of communication. It makes for good entertainment (like Obi-Wan telling Luke that his father was killed by Darth Vader), but not being forthcoming with our partners out of self-preservation or the idea that we're noble and protecting them usually results in more harm than good.

We've all watched people in our lives make this particular mistake and we saw the bad consequences coming from a mile away. It's so crazy they didn't see it themselves, right? Like secretive behavior leading to mistaken assumptions about infidelity. Or someone not sharing a medical diagnosis with their family leading to regret and resentment and lost time in finding a solution, sometimes with devastating results.

But unfortunate things like these don't have to happen if you just *talk about it*. And right now, "it" is whatever your partner is going through that is shaking their world up a little.

You may think, "They already tell me everything so this doesn't apply to me." I certainly felt that way with Brett prior to "the big change" but from experience I can assure you that your typical relationship dynamics don't automatically apply in this situation because it's new for everyone. You really do need to explicitly bring up this topic of conversation every once in a while.

At least your partner has confided in you. Unfortunately, there are many people out there still hiding their development from their partners because they're afraid of the reaction they'll get. But even though they've opened up to you partially, they might be keeping some important details from you in a misguided attempt to spare you from the discomfort they're feeling or to protect themselves, out of fear that you'll think they're crazy if they really get into it.

Ask them, "So have you seen/heard/felt anything lately?" "What's happening with 'that stuff' these days?" "This is really interesting so you have to tell me if something new pops up."

Make sure to explicitly extend these types of supportive and nonjudgmental invitations occasionally, to give them opportunities to elaborate on their perceptions and experiences. Then really listen with as much compassion and openness as you can muster. You have to seem receptive to at least hearing what they have to say, even if the details are hard for you to accept at first.

Eventually, discussion about this new aspect of your life will become automatic, like talking about what happened at work that day. And in fact, talking about the concepts that are currently difficult to wrap your mind around will someday probably seem as commonplace as trying to agree on what to have for dinner. But in the beginning your loved one may need reassurance and convincing that they are safe telling even you about the unusual ideas going on in their head.

And just because they tell you what's happening doesn't mean you will truly understand what's happening (or even that they understand what's happening), but at this point that's not of supreme importance. What you're doing is strengthening your relationship by being willing to hear about how their world is being shaken up and how they feel about it all.

Sadly, this friendly ear and receptivity are more than many people in such situations receive from their family and friends. These simple acts of connecting and accepting will keep your bond strong and will give you some leverage in case you need it in the future.

Ask specifically what they need from you

Don't just assume that you know what kind of support your loved one needs at any particular time, even if you have a long relationship history. Their worldview may be shifting, causing the ground beneath their feet to feel unstable. The strong person you've known for so many years might feel uncharacteristically vulnerable right now. (Or alternately, invulnerable, which has its own set of potential issues.)

Brett sometimes wants to be left alone. Sometimes he wants the comfort of physical contact. Sometimes he wants to hear what I think about what he's telling me, but sometimes not. I have to figure it out and he doesn't mind if I ask. In fact, he feels respected and loved when I ask and it makes my job easier.

Some people have a hard time asking for or accepting any kind of help so if your partner is one of them, you'll have to use those skills you've honed over the years to get past the "I'm fine" responses when they are obviously not fine. This is too important for them to struggle with alone, and you want to keep it clear that you are their biggest supporter.

On the other hand, some people need time alone to process their thoughts and emotions before they're ready to discuss them in a coherent way. I know a guy (a new psychic) who sits alone in silence after work, integrating his metaphysical experiences into his rapidly changing worldview. He'll sit there sometimes for two or three hours and it drives his girlfriend crazy.

She always wants to talk about it, so she's on track there, but she's having to learn to tolerate when he's not ready to talk *yet*. He usually appreciates her initial query into his state of mind but then seems annoyed when she can't leave him alone due to her own insecurity. Part of effectively asking what someone needs is accepting and respecting the answer we get.

Over time you'll learn to pick up on their subtle and not-so-subtle "tells." Behaviors like them sitting in a room with no TV, radio, or computer on, if that's uncharacteristic. Wanting to be closer to or farther away from others than usual. A level of agitation in their voice that typically only happens when they're feeling stressed. Or perhaps the opposite—too much cheeriness that you know is probably masking anxiety. The signs are different for each person and the best response to each scenario is equally as personal. But you'll figure the patterns out and at that point you can start acting mostly on auto-pilot, like you've probably done for so long.

Until then, just don't assume anything.

Do your research

Knowledge is power. Since you seem to be a book reader, perhaps a memoir by someone who has successfully weathered the emergence of psychic ability will help you (and by extension, your partner) better understand what is going on.

Fortunately, they are abundant. An Amazon search of the very specific term "psychic memoir" returns over 600 results, with 9,000 for "mediumship" and 60,000 hits for the more general "psychic." Public libraries usually have at least a couple of these titles available.

Chapter 10, "Don't Just Take My Word for It," is a good place to start. It provides several short accounts from people who share what helped and didn't help during their own psychic development phases.

There is seemingly endless information on the internet and as you probably noticed when looking for this book, there are new books being published almost daily about psychic ability and paranormal phenomena. This alone should tell you how prevalent it is becoming in our society.

I am fortunate that I was already interested in this subject in a general way when it came time for me to start digging around. That made it feel more like a pastime than a dreaded school project. My hope is that you, too, are curious in this area or at least enjoy learning new things so doing research doesn't feel like chore.

You'll have plenty of options and angles to choose from when looking for information to help your partner. Pragmatic approaches, fluffy approaches, esoteric approaches, advanced approaches, beginner approaches. One is not better than the other. Just find what makes sense to you today. Tomorrow a different approach might appeal instead and that's OK. In the spiritual community we use the word "resonate" to describe when something feels right to us. Find what resonates with you and follow that trail until you're moved to look for something else.

Your loved one may already be well versed on the subject and that's great. They may come up with all of the information they actually need on their own. But as you've guessed by now, the value of your involvement isn't just that you are another set of eyes scouring the world wide web for the most accurate and digestible data. You are demonstrating that you are a partner in this experience with them. That you support their process. That you accept what they are telling you as true, or at least as their truth. That you want to understand what is happening to them instead of rejecting or denying it.

Keep an open mind

Mysticism, healing, and related abilities have been great and noble traditions throughout human history. Psychology, in the form of Jung's collective unconscious and the modalities of transpersonal and spiritual psychology, lends credence to these phenomena, as well. Even quantum physics is increasingly bridging the gap between the mundane and the metaphysical.

Well-known psychic Chip Coffey, in his book *Growing Up Psychic*, puts things into perspective for us by saying, "Being psychic is simply having the ability to…receive information that cannot be accessed using the five human senses." He's right, and when we look at it this way we realize there's no reason to be any more afraid of people with these skills than of people who understand high-level mathematical concepts that are over most of our heads.

We are fortunate that our society is finally waking up to the prevalence and in a sense, normalness of so-called supernatural abilities. Your current situation may be your initial introduction to such phenomena, but I assure you that you pass some ordinary-seeming people on the street every day who have their own hidden bag of tricks.

Studies by CBS and Gallup (and others) show that more than half of Americans admit to believing in psychic ability. Perhaps you already do, too. However, it's often hard to accept that something so incredible is happening to someone close to us, even when we believe in it in general. But you need to be able to accept that what your partner is sharing is a truthful recounting of their actual experience and to proceed accordingly (even if you think they may be mistaken).

If you're having trouble tolerating the claims your partner is making, remind yourself that there are many people who know a lot more than you do about science, music, working out, military tactics, etc., and you wouldn't be rude to them or dismiss information they're sharing just because it pushed the boundaries of your knowledge base. Since the person we're talking about is one of the people you care about most in the world, you need to afford them at least the level of respect you would give a stranger in hearing what they have to say.

When someone is learning an academic subject we don't expect them to master it right away. We give them leeway to develop their knowledge and skills in stages, so we need to do that here, too.

I can warn you from personal experience that it's tempting to use any inconsistencies against them in the beginning. Just don't. Try to remember that the full accuracy of the information isn't of prime importance at this point. *Your #1 goal is to maintain or even improve the relationship through your handling of the situation.*

Don't let your discomfort or reactivity become a wedge between you. Keep your mind open and bite your tongue if you feel the urge to argue, dismiss, or condescend. Not arguing doesn't mean you agree with everything they're saying. You're just giving them time and space to figure out a subject that might be completely foreign to them at this point.

Express yourself well

When we are faced with new stressors, we can sometimes become desperate and frustrated. It's easy to resort to angry, hurtful words in order to try to reestablish our sense of power and control. Such an out-of-this-world scenario certainly qualifies as a trigger for saying things we might regret later because we don't know what else to do.

When you're feeling overwhelmed or threatened by what your partner is saying, it's dangerously easy to lash out with comments like "I knew you'd turn out crazy like your mother." "My friends told me not to marry you. I should've backed out when I had the chance." "You don't know what you're talking about." "You're just imagining that." "You're delusional."

We know each others' buttons and sometimes it's mighty tempting to push them. Either directly or passive aggressively. Sometimes it's blatant but sometimes it manifests as a steady stream of snide comments disguised as good-natured joking, with each one seeming relatively harmless by itself but taken in combination, betraying a buried sense of hostility or resentment.

Behaving in this manner is always counterproductive. It will create distance between you, which actually means you have less power and control, defeating your own purpose. Someone who is being judged, criticized, or undermined usually digs into their position instead of listening to what you have to say. So by losing your cool, you're actually relinquishing whatever amount of power you had in the first place.

But more importantly, treating each other in such an unloving and disrespectful way erodes your relationship tremendously. In all cases, regardless of circumstances. But in this particular context, where insecurity is already a major player, such harshness and contempt can cause irreparable damage.

Of course you are *always* entitled to have feelings and needs, though, and this situation is no exception. Just remember to use the "I" language that helps keep communication productive. You know, statements that reflect your own thoughts and experiences instead of suggesting that the other person is wrong in some way.

- I'm feeling kind of overwhelmed by all of this right now. Can we talk about it later?
- I'm having trouble understanding what you're telling me because I've never experienced anything like that before.
- I'm scared that this is going to impact our life together.

Come to think of it, these three statements encompass almost all of the upset feelings that might arise in relation to your partner developing psychic/healing/mediumship abilities. By using these models you could generate an "I" message to express any of your concerns.

- I'm worried about how this stuff is going to impact the children/your job/our place in the community.

- I know this is really important but I have a ton of things to take care of right now. Can we talk about this later when I have time to listen?
- I know you're telling me the truth about what you saw, but it's hard for me to digest because it's different than what I was raised to believe.

In healthy relationships, this type of honest vulnerability is welcome and often results in a stronger connection because it creates the opportunity for your partner to support you, even as you support them. Being able to fulfill someone's authentic, reasonable needs is satisfying and good for self-esteem. (This is why, in contrast, being in a relationship with a "needy" person is so exhausting and unsatisfying. The fact that their needs can never be filled leaves the partner feeling impotent.)

In the process of regulating your emotions, you will have to decide what to say to your loved one and what to save for your own support network. (We'll talk more about support for you in Chapter 8.) Always remember that you're trying to work as a team to find the best solutions and make the best possible life together. If what you feel compelled to say does not serve that end then you should probably hold off or find somewhere more productive to express it.

Even without any unusual elements in your relationship, it's not always best to just say everything that's on your mind when you're upset. You've heard "Don't promise when you're happy, don't reply when you're angry, don't decide when you're sad," right? That applies here, too.

If you have to get something off your chest in a moment of utter desperation, write it down, then burn it to let it go. Or write it in a journal. Do whatever you need to do to process upset feelings privately so they don't come out in the wrong way.

But the cardinal rule is never ever badmouth your partner to your family, your in-laws, your kids, any mutual friends, in public, or on social media. Of course this applies across the board, not just in this situation.

Learn to hear what is really being said

A helpful and relevant skill I learned in my psych training program was separating the information contained in a message from the energy of that message. For example, when people are angry and yelling at us, we tend to become defensive and reject everything they're saying. But it is possible to hear the spoken and unspoken messages without becoming engaged with someone's emotionality, and we can almost always learn something valuable from what they're trying to say.

Becoming less reactive during challenging communication actually puts us in a power position because we are operating from greater self-control and are therefore being less controlled by outside sources. Being willing to hear the part of someone's message that may be useful, regardless of their behavior, is a demonstration of self-mastery and maturity.

So when you feel yourself getting anxious, upset, or otherwise emotional over some "nonsense" your loved one is telling you, remind yourself that emotions are just energy and you can let those go. Focus on getting the message without the distraction of reaction.

Don't forget that laughter really is the best medicine
We know that laughter/humor:
- Diffuses tension and diminishes a sense of threat
- Makes undesirable feedback more palatable to receive
- Increases endorphins (happiness hormones)
- Relieves physical pain and improves immunity
- Tends to keep someone's interest longer than serious communication styles

Consequently, sense of humor is pretty high up on most people's lists of what they appreciate about others—especially a romantic partner. Inside jokes are one example of how humor is a great bonding mechanism. The experience of finding the same thing funny leads to a feeling of deeper connection.

In your relationship you've probably already determined where the line is between "joking about something" and "acting like something is a joke." It's a useful distinction. You don't want to cross that line but you definitely want to play on the respectful side of it, when appropriate.

A few weeks ago Brett and I were talking to a couple who are new to all of this psychic stuff and are having frequent poltergeist activity in their apartment. The conversation got heavier and heavier as they described their sense of being overwhelmed in their own home, but then the man decided to tell their "false alarm" story.

On a night that had been especially busy with paranormal weirdness, there was one final straw. When he came back inside from having a cigarette at 2 a.m., it appeared that something he had previously thrown away had rematerialized in his living room. He sat awake on the couch until sunrise, fearing he might lose his mind, assuming that spirits were taunting him in a way that he couldn't guard his family against. When morning came, he gathered up his courage and explained the situation to his wife, who he expected to be equally distraught. Only it turns out she had previously purchased an exact duplicate of the item and had put it out in the living room while he was having a cigarette.

This guy is a great story teller so he built up the drama of his near breakdown in such a way that we were all bent over with laughter by the end. The release of tension through humor was exactly what they needed to regain a sense that things were manageable and they were able to go home feeling like themselves again.

Embrace naturally occurring laughter to keep life fresh and light. This applies to all situations at all times, of course, but especially during a period of growth that may sometimes feel heavy or confusing. Ideally, all parties involved will find ways to pack humor (including self-deprecating humor) into their coping-mechanism toolbox.

And who knows, by maintaining a good attitude you might just find that all of this is genuinely fun at least part of the time.

Don't ask them to perform

Certainly it might be hard to accept that our husbands or wives can see or do whatever it is they are making claims to. It's tempting to want them to prove that they can read our past lives, do energy healing, or talk to our deceased grandmothers. And at some point they may be able to do so, but it has to be at their discretion, on their own timeline.

These abilities, especially in the beginning, can be intermittent or erratic. They are often less accessible or effective if the person is "trying too hard." Setting up a situation where your loved one becomes even more stressed out by pressure you are putting on them is potentially damaging to their mental health (remember—they're probably struggling with this new reality already anyway) and is definitely not good for your relationship.

At this point, their demonstration probably won't meet the expectations you would have for a professional psychic or one you see on TV anyway. Those people are often highly skilled and have had years of practice, sometimes a lifetime. It's not fair to compare a beginner to a pro in any field. It's normal that a newcomer can't compete with the performance standards of someone with much more experience. And the fact that 99% of people can't be in the top 1% in any particular field doesn't mean they don't have some legitimate talent. So cut your partner some slack.

It's also sometimes harder to effectively read or work on a person that you already know because too much information can interfere with your results, so this may impact their ability to give you what you're looking for at first. This might seem counterintuitive, as if working on a person you're close to should be easier because of your comfort level with them, but it just doesn't play out that way.

Therefore, the right way to handle your desire for "proof" is to express eagerness to be shown what they're doing when they're "on" or "in the flow." Let them know you're not going to judge their performance but just want to be included because this is an important part of your life together.

Give them credit for small "hits" (accurate psychic perceptions). Don't try to find ways to dismiss their hits as coincidence, lucky guesses, etc. There's a sense of vulnerability in daring to share psychic impressions with another person in the beginning so don't abuse your power position.

If you are genuinely looking for an opportunity to support them and are not just being a naysayer or devil's advocate, you will eventually get the validation you seek (if their abilities are legitimate). It will be another of many bonding moments afforded by this process. You can be impressed, they can feel good. It's a win-win when it finally happens.

Understand that the world may feel different to them now

Even if your loved one is a rock in general, he or she can be in a strangely fragile position when psychic abilities are first manifesting. Certain environments and situations that used to be comfortable and appealing may now be uncomfortable or even unbearable for them. You will have to accept that maybe they can't do everything they used to do, at least temporarily.

A common example is that your significant other might now be hypersensitive to crowds because they can feel everyone's emotional energy. And that just means you'll have to go to the mall or concert or county fair with someone else until they get it under control, if it's that important to you.

Brett went through a period of about a year when he couldn't watch any fantasy, sci-fi, or scary movies. The imagery was just too disturbing to him because he had interacted with many entities that looked or felt like the Hollywood aliens, monsters, and ghosts in his psychic sessions, and seeing them looming large on the screen caused something like a PTSD reaction in him.

This was a huge disappointment to me because most blockbusters now fall into those genres so we were rarely able to go to the movies together during that time period (which felt dreadfully long). But of course I had to respect his heightened sensitivity. So for a while I got a new movie buddy for the big-screen spectacles and for the rest I just waited until I could watch them at home.

Hey, I never said there weren't sacrifices involved in this process, just that by making the best of your circumstances you can come out on top.

It's a bummer to lose some of the activities you used to enjoy doing together but your relationship will actually become more intimate than ever so the payoff for being understanding and supportive is worthwhile. By respecting and accepting their needs, however unusual, you are growing closer even when you aren't always participating together.

And it creates an opening for you to do more activities with friends, which is not only enjoyable but is great for stress relief.

Be a buffer

It's also important to be a buffer by helping them figure out plausible excuses for turning down invitations to their previously preferred activities, in cases where telling the truth isn't the smartest approach. You don't need to offend a host by saying you're staying away from their house because you've realized their neediness or moodiness takes too much of a toll on your partner. Or maybe you want to. I guess it really depends on your personality. But you definitely don't need to give away any of the family secrets when your sensitive loved one needs to avoid something.

As natural introverts, people weren't terribly surprised when we declined invitations to a lot of events anyway. But if your loved one has traditionally been very social and outgoing, you'll want to develop a catalog of believable, non-worrying reasons why they aren't going to be around as often as they used to be for a while.

The goals, of course, are for the person in spiritual emergence to return to the healthy parts of their typical functioning as quickly as possible and hopefully also grow in positive ways from their experiences. But for the short term, be aware of and responsive to their temporary limitations by not forcing or pressuring them. Just branch out on your own, without resentment, when you really want to do something that doesn't work for them.

Learn sign language

Something that can be fun during this phase is figuring out your private language so you can communicate about what's happening without others catching on. It's not much different from having your secret cues to each other that you're ready to leave a party, or the brief glances that you instantly understand between yourselves but that others wouldn't even notice.

Also there will be events that occur repeatedly so you'll want to have a shorthand way of talking about them. This will probably develop naturally, as your other modes of unique, intimate communication have throughout the course of your relationship.

I'm not going to give away our specific catalog of hand signals because these are for you to create on your own, just between the two of you. But I will say that Brett and I can tell each other what we're experiencing without anyone else noticing, which is useful and strengthens the feeling of being a cohesive team. It's also kind of amusing to be sharing "secrets" right in front of others.

As brief examples, we have hand gestures we make that refer to "being touched," "seeing something," "hearing something," and "other." Honestly, we've never used "other" and I don't really know what that would refer to but we just wanted to be thorough.

Another example that's not sign language but still falls into the category of creating your own lexicon is that we used to call a certain type of entity "the August people" because they first showed up one year in August. We didn't want to refer to them by name because we thought that doing so would attract their attention. We don't use that term anymore and are just frank about them when they're around (which is less often than it used to be, thankfully), but it was necessary at first so we could talk in front of others who weren't "on to us" yet.

So you can see that it doesn't even have to make sense to anyone but you. Have fun designing your own unique vocabulary. Make sure it's practical and easy to remember.

Play it close to the vest at first

Pregnancy, starting a new business, emerging psychic abilities—these life events are generally best shared only with a small, trusted inner circle until the change or endeavor is solidly established and you have come to terms with what it really means for your life.

Most people are well meaning but if they haven't experienced a particular life change personally, their advice can be more annoying than helpful. Judgmental parenting advice from people without kids. Time-wasting micromanagement from a boss who has no background in your line of work. Back-seat drivers. Who needs any of that?

And some people are not even well meaning and will intentionally use this kind of information to try to undermine your self-confidence, relationship, or position in the community. So just keep this new development fairly private in the beginning.

Now let me tell you something you may need to hear: You don't have to feel guilty about keeping this information to yourselves for a while! Truly, nobody outside of your nuclear family has any legitimate claim to know your most intimate personal business anyway. I know social media, nosy neighbors, and meddling in-laws might try to convince you otherwise, but maintaining a degree of privacy is actually a healthy psychological practice.

If the person experiencing psychic development is reacting by wanting to tell too many people too quickly, try to rein them in. It can be painful and disheartening to share news with people whose opinions you value if they don't react the way you want them to, so discourage your partner from risking it until they're strong enough to weather any response.

Even telling someone like a therapist, doctor, or clergy member is not necessarily a productive approach because people in their professional roles, on average, will dismiss psychic/healing abilities and merely try to provide an alternate explanation that fits within the narrowly defined worldview of their particular training. Even if they believe in psychic ability or paranormal phenomena on a personal level, their professional guidelines and/or reputation within their field often requires them, explicitly or implicitly, to categorize your experiences otherwise.

I know a woman who took her elementary-aged son to a therapist because he was having upsetting visions that would later come true. She hoped it would help her son deal with the emotional roller coaster he was experiencing as a result of his ability. But quickly the mother realized the counselor's treatment plan was to disabuse the family of the idea that anything unusual was happening. He considered it just a case of a child's imagination being irresponsibly overindulged.

Fortunately, the boy was too young to catch on to any of the subtle derision from the therapist and of course the mother stopped taking the boy to sessions immediately. But what if he or his mother had sought the support of a school-based psychologist or someone within their insurance network? The mental health professional's opinion that the boy had detoured from reality would have been recorded on a permanent file that would follow the child well into adulthood.

This tendency toward reductionism, called "medical materialism" when applied to the medical field, has been discussed as a problem for over a century. I'll get into more detail about this in Chapter 4, where I break down the argument for "psychic vs. psychotic."

Only you can be the judge of whether someone in your life is truly open minded and objective enough to be included on your support team in the early stages. Don't assume that because someone generally provides good advice for typical life challenges means that they will be able to do the same in this unusual case. Will it actually be helpful for you or your loved one for this person to know, or might it cause more problems than it solves?

Just be thoughtful in your evaluation on a case-by-case basis and don't "spill the beans" impulsively.

If you're feeling like you want to talk to someone about it, consider easing your way up to the full conversation. By gauging their reactions to things like TV shows about ghost hunting or the latest celebrity psychic, you'll know how ready they are to hear what you have to say.

Help them craft the message

Our loved ones need to feel like they can express themselves, but in such novel circumstances they might not have the ability to correctly analyze what is appropriate to share with whom and how to phrase it in a way that it will be well received. They need our help, and it is important that we have accepted (hopefully, embraced) the situation adequately in order to be a loving voice of reason.

The first time Brett told any of our coworkers about his abilities and how we spend some of our free time (e.g. checking houses for hostile entities, energy healing, communicating with animals), he basically spilled *everything*. Every seemingly absurd thing. Things that took us a long time to wrap our minds around. Things that actually require some background knowledge to comprehend. He told it all in one rushed conversation because he'd been wanting desperately to tell them for so long.

Fortunately, he had a long-term, mutually respectful relationship with these people and they already knew he was "a little different" so they mostly accepted and believed him, but only to the degree that they could even understand what he was talking about.

I found his approach not ideal and possibly even counterproductive, but all I could do was appreciate his enthusiasm for connecting with our coworkers on a deeper level and focus on helping him figure out a better way to express himself in the future.

We discussed each element, considering what the average listener could tolerate or understand and what he should omit completely. We played with different ways of explaining his abilities and though he was eager to share all of his newfound knowledge with everybody he cared about (and really, anybody else who would listen), together we were able to construct a workable mental catalog of explanations and descriptions.

You can be certain, though, that this would not have worked had I not been very diligent in showing him that I accepted his experience and was on his team 100%. If he had felt that I was merely trying to censor him, he would not have been able to receive my suggestions with an open mind.

We can take a lesson from marketing when figuring out how to talk about this stuff. We should prepare a variety of ways to communicate our ideas so that any particular audience can understand.

We need our "elevator pitch," which means the 5- or 20-second version that allows a casual listener to walk away feeling like they got the general idea without being overwhelmed or bored.

- I'm a medium (which means I can talk to/see dead people).
- I'm an energy healer (which means I can remove stagnant energy and infuse healthy energy into your body so it functions better).
- I'm an animal communicator (which means I can talk to animals telepathically; they do this with each other all the time already anyway).

This is really all the information that most people, especially those not close to you, are going to want. They can go home and tell someone, "I met a medium today" and either have their curiosity privately piqued by the concept or laugh at it. Either way it doesn't really affect us.

Take heart in knowing that as you and partner become more and more comfortable with the message yourselves, you will be less and less impacted by how well it is received by detractors or closed-minded people.

But don't underestimate the acceptance and great interest in the esoteric these days. During jury duty just last month I stated my spouse's occupation as "medium," expecting to hear some snickering from the other panelists. Instead, another juror asked me for Brett's card because he wanted a reading.

For the most part, close family and friends, even those who are unbelievers, are just going to want to know that everything is OK, so figure out a way to make what's happening as light and non-threatening as possible in those cases.

Some will want to know a lot more, though, so we also need to be prepared to answer at greater length, in more detail. When someone is able to ask on-point questions about the process it usually means they already have background knowledge, which makes them a good audience and you can open up a little more. They may not even need basic explanations but are just interested in the unique way that your partner is experiencing the phenomenon.

Here are some questions that truly interested people typically have, for which you should help your loved one develop some workable answers.

How do you know what you know? Usually what they want to know with these types of questions is what sensory perception is working for this particular psychic. Does he/she hear a voice that gives them information? If so, does it sound like their own voice or someone else's? Do they see spirits physically with their eyes or just in their "mind's eye?" Figure out how to explain the actual input mechanisms in a way that's easy to understand. Many people are fascinated by this kind of stuff and are excited to have someone to discuss it with. (For a list of psychic modalities, see Chapter 9.)

When/how did this start? You could just say "in June" but if they're asking at all, they generally want more of a story than that. Did the abilities come on gradually or in a sudden or even traumatic fashion? What was the first real experience you can recall that convinced you things were changing? Remember that more and more people are having psychic and paranormal experiences so sometimes when we're asked about our situation, the person is secretly looking for validation. You're actually giving them a gift by being willing and able to talk about it.

How do you know it's not just your imagination/you're not just crazy? Some people will ask in mockery, and we mostly just blow those people off because no amount of proof or reasoning is going to change a skeptic's mind. Don't bother arguing and don't take the limitations of their thinking as a reflection on you or your partner. Everyone has to figure it out in their own time.

But some will be asking out of genuine curiosity or concern so try to have a solid response prepared. Figuring out how to answer this question for others is a great exercise for yourselves, as well.

Corroboration by another source/person is typically the most convincing evidence. Whenever I can speak up that I witnessed something, too, or had a similar experience, it forces people to consider that it might be more than Brett's imagination. Or at least it makes them rationalize to themselves that we're both either mistaken or lying.

And depending on who you're talking to, it will be either the conviction of your own belief in your experiences or to the contrary, how dispassionately and "scientifically" you can talk about your experiences that will do a better job of convincing them. You can either change your presentation based on who the audience is, or just give your spiel and let them take it or leave it.

It's essential to learn to tolerate and accept people's disbelief. After all, what you're trying to convince them of maybe seemed like fantasy to you not so long ago, too.

Even after all these years, Brett and I are still working on culling, honing, and tweaking how we share this information with others. Some things that make perfect sense to us, because we're living it, leave people with their heads slightly cocked and a glimmer of confusion in their eyes. Other things we talk about are clearly understood but seem to cause in the listener a subtle (or not so subtle) change in stance to that of dismissive, incredulous, or downright scared.

We are perpetually trying to figure out how to talk about this stuff in a way that leaves people feeling uplifted and educated, if they have a mind to be so. I imagine it will be a lifelong process and is really more about learning how to gauge what people want and need than just having the technically correct words to describe the ability or experience.

Does psychic ability run in your family? You may assume not, but do you really know? Maybe it does and everybody's just too scared to talk about it.

Can you do a healing/reading for me? Your partner will encounter so many people who want to receive the benefits of their psychic ability, and often for free. Working *pro bono* for the rest of their life is totally fine as long as they have another source of income. But it's also a good idea to have some answers ready for when they don't want to (or can't) work on someone.

Maybe your partner will never, ever want to use their ability that way. Also totally fine. They don't have to prove to anything to anyone and they don't owe anyone anything. Just help them be prepared to respond to this request because they'll get it a lot.

Be prepared to lose some of your privacy

Be forewarned: Once the information gets out, you're going to lose some degree of privacy. I just want to you to be really clear on this before you decide to go around telling people.

Psychic ability—like veganism, yoga, homeschooling, or a medical condition—may become a big part of your life, but it isn't necessarily what you should lead with when introduced to people. Depending on the crowd, of course. In some circumstances it's completely fine. Or if you're the kind of person who likes to push people's buttons and comfort zones, go for it. I just want to make sure you're aware of the possible outcomes and how they can affect your life.

The increased attention you get might be almost negligible, or it might be very noticeable, to the point of disruptive. Regardless of where you live, you'll get some positive reactions and some negative. You'll probably make some new interesting, enlightened friends, but be prepared to lose some old friends who can't handle it.

As I mentioned earlier, your partner will likely get requests for psychic work from people in the neighborhood. He/she might even be asked to interview for a local publication. Getting threatening notes in your mailbox from someone down the street who thinks that all psychic ability and paranormal phenomena are evil is not out of the question. Good-natured teasing from co-workers is likely. Your kids getting some not-so-good-natured teasing from classmates (because kids can be cruel) is also not unlikely. Under some circumstances, revealing this information might even affect your jobs.

Or on the other hand, the people around you might be thoroughly disinterested and unaffected by your revelation. This is a relief and a blessing in some cases but a disappointment in others, depending on what kind of reaction we're hoping for.

But this potential for attention and reactivity from your community is why I emphasize keeping your experience close to the vest until you're both ready to handle whatever may come.

This is also why it's so important for each of you to establish new support networks of people who are going through similar experiences, to offset the potential discomfort that comes from any skeptics, naysayers, or critics who surface once you've relinquished your privacy in this regard. I will discuss this more in later chapters.

We didn't tell our coworkers at the school or even part of our family about Brett's abilities for many years. To our pleasant surprise, almost everyone we've eventually shared this information with has either had some experience themselves or has at least been very supportive of us.

Yet despite that positive response to our "reveal," we still don't talk about it with just everyone we meet or even everyone we've known for a long time if we're not close to them and they seem unreceptive. It's not that we're hiding, we just don't care to try to convince anyone or defend ourselves to people who don't get it.

Don't forget to take care of the most important person—YOU

You might be feeling like your partner's ascent into psychic functioning is a great adventure. On the other hand you might feel kind of bitter that all of a sudden there's an imbalance in the equilibrium between you. Maybe you're a little jealous of the cool stuff they're able to do now. Or maybe you resent that their issues are disrupting your previously comfortable life.

All of that is OK. You are entitled to your feelings. I realize that up until this point I've focused an awful lot on what your loved one needs so just hold on—Chapter 8 is dedicated to "Taking Care of Yourself." I'll talk exclusively about YOU—what you can do to minimize your stress and some ways you can enjoy this ride. You need to continue making the most of your own life while also lifting up your significant other.

But first, let's get serious for a minute and discuss the differences between psychic ability and psychosis, just in case you're worried about that.

Chapter 4

BUT WHAT IF THEY'RE JUST CRAZY?

The information contained in this chapter (and this book in general) is for basic educational purposes only. It is not intended to be a substitute for professional medical/psychiatric advice, diagnosis, or treatment. Any time your loved one is experiencing noticeable changes in functioning or behavior it's a good idea to get a physical check-up to make sure everything is still in order.

My hope for you is that your loved one has been able to demonstrate, at least to your minimal satisfaction, that they do indeed possess some new gift or ability, and therefore your concerns about their mental health (in this particular scenario) have been adequately relieved.

But even under the best of circumstances it is sometimes difficult for us to accept that these largely intangible phenomena are really happening. That's why I've chosen to include this chapter about the differences between psychosis and psychic ability.

Being eccentric is not a diagnosable trait

First off, in order to qualify for a diagnosis of one of the psychotic disorders (or any other disorder for that matter), the person in question must meet several criteria, usually including "Social/Occupational Dysfunction," which is often worded this way in the *DSM (Diagnostic and Statistical Manual*—the psychiatrists' and insurance companies' bible of what they think is wrong with people):

> *For a significant portion of the time since the onset of the disturbance, one or more major areas of functioning, such as work, interpersonal relations, or self-care, are markedly below the level achieved prior to the onset.*

Additionally, NAMI (the National Alliance for the Mentally Ill—the largest grassroots mental health organization in the U.S.) defines mental illness as "a medical condition that often results in a diminished capacity for coping with the ordinary demands of life."

Therefore, even if you find it thoroughly unbelievable that someone is talking to dead people, having premonitions about impending catastrophes, or healing others through meditation or prayer, that does not mean it would qualify them for a psychotic disorder diagnosis.

So really, the question is: can they actually no longer function in the world or do they just claim or demonstrate an extra talent now?

If there's no major functional impairment and the issue is that you are uncomfortable with this new development, I am sorry to say that it falls upon you to process this life change for your own peace of mind instead of trying to pathologize a behavior just because you don't like or understand it.

Would a label even be helpful?

In many books about psychic ability you will find a reference to the misapplication of *disorder du jour* labels by society to psychically adept individuals. Especially children.

In my personal experience of working with college-bound special needs students for almost 20 years, I've seen a higher-than-average proportion of kids with "ADD/ADHD" and "Emotionally Disturbed" labels on their special ed paperwork who also have psychic gifts (which, understandably, are not listed on their special ed paperwork).

For example, one of our high school students, IQ off the charts, would be fine for a few months then he would start to have episodes of not sleeping for days or even weeks. This would produce in him the expected results of sleep deprivation: emotional instability, difficulty focusing, diminished capacity for clear communication, and sleeping in class (which in some less-understanding environments would have been viewed as defiance).

This young man had seen psychiatrists who put him on various sleep-aids and he had even participated in a couple sleep studies by the time he was 16. All of these medical professionals together arrived at the brilliant (non-)diagnosis of just "insomnia" (and later, "sleep paralysis"). With all of their collective education and experience, that's the best they could come up with.

During one of his recovery phases from a particularly rough and long episode, this student stopped into my office just to say hi. I always kept my door open at the school because much of the most important work with teenagers happens spontaneously and on their timeline.

So I welcomed the boy in, and even though there was another boy (relatively new to the school and also exceptionally bright) already in my office, I took the opportunity to ask why he had so much trouble sleeping.

"I have insomnia."

"Yes, but insomnia is just a symptom. Why do you have insomnia?"

He paused and I could tell he was deliberating about whether to tell me his truth or not. Despite the fact that the students didn't know about my wacky extracurricular activities, I still had a reputation for being open minded, so I guess he decided to give it a shot.

"Because sometimes there are shadow people in my room trying to talk to me and I'm scared and they won't let me sleep," he mumbled.

Before I could respond with an accepting, comforting word, the new boy turned around from his computer and said, "Push your bed against the wall. Sleep facing the wall so you can't see them. And always sleep on your stomach because that's how they try to get in."

Neither boy was joking. I doubt they ever mentioned it to each other again, if they ever even spoke to each other about anything at all beyond that point.

But here were two fantastically bright young men, having similar "crazy" experiences, and it was impacting their lives significantly enough that they couldn't function in public school. And they didn't feel like they could talk to anybody about it.

Over the years, how many doctors and other adults had my severely sleep-deprived student discussed his insomnia with but not admitted to them what was happening out of a fear of being labeled mentally ill? How many of those adults had he confided in, only to be told his perceptions were not valid? And how much more productive could this really intelligent young man have been if he wasn't living with constant anxiety and in a destructive cycle of trying to manage these terrifying experiences alone?

As of this writing, he was still trying to figure out how to regulate himself and manifest his high potential. By comparison, the other young man eventually told his mother about his experiences and she responded in a supportive manner. She even accompanied him to a weekend workshop about incorporating spirituality and metaphysics into a healthy, satisfying life. This second young man is now thriving in college and I expect he will make a lasting positive impact on the world.

From the abundance of cases just like these we can draw two conclusions: Either psychic sensitivity is misdiagnosed and given more mainstream labels; or psychic sensitivity and these "Disorders Usually First Diagnosed in Infancy, Childhood or Adolescence" (a category from the *DSM-IV*) have a high degree of co-occurrence (meaning they frequently happen together). I feel confident that both are true.

Therefore, if you are going to have your loved one evaluated for a diagnosis, at the very least be sure to find a specialist who acknowledges the existence of both mental illness and psychic ability so they can determine which one applies (if not both).

And be sure that having the diagnosis is going to be beneficial overall. If a person's functioning is impaired to the point that pharmacological treatment would improve their daily life, then assessment by a professional is certainly warranted.

But be warned that there are significant lifelong ramifications of receiving a mental illness diagnosis and/or being medicated. Please do weigh the usefulness of entering into this process very carefully.

Visions vs. hallucinations/delusions

I'm not saying there's no such thing as legitimate schizophrenia or other psychotic conditions, I'm just trying to show you how spiritual, mystical, and paranormal experiences are quite distinct from mental illness. And how such esoteric phenomena are also quite common.

A rough indicator of the difference between psychic ability (even if it strikes you as crazy) and actual psychosis is the nature of their visions (or delusions, in the case of schizophrenia).

The schizophrenic patterns I'm referring to specifically are called "delusions of persecution" and "delusions of reference."

For example, while well-informed citizens and conspiracy theorists alike know that the government is up to sneaky stuff, a schizophrenic person is likely to think that such activities are directed specifically at them. They sometimes believe that strangers are watching them and orchestrating events in order to create a staged reality just for them. And whereas any of us would probably accept the possibility of subliminal messages in advertising, a schizophrenic person is likely to argue that there is information embedded intended solely for them.

I've worked with students and adult clients with these delusional thought patterns so I know there really are plenty of people suffering with these psychological burdens.

To the contrary, when a psychic sees an event that relates to others they don't try to make it be about themselves. If they see auras, they understand that auras are there all the time; it's not that the person lit up just to get their attention. When a psychometrist (see Chapter 9 for definitions of different types of psychic ability) touches an object, the information they receive relates completely to the owner of that item, not to themselves. You get the idea.

One type of personal information that psychics do receive is communication from their Spirit Guides, who I discussed briefly in the previous chapter. Your Guides are focused on you alone and will give you answers that are only supportive and helpful in nature. They are your cheerleaders and they aren't going to tell you to do anything that will jeopardize your human or soul success (or anyone else's).

When your partner gets guidance from these entities, it should always be leading to positive action or feelings. Brett got a strong message to stop drinking coffee so he did and it cleared up his fragrance allergy. Who would've guessed those were related? Certainly no doctor or allergist I've talked to.

When the information is positive in nature, the odds are good that what they're experiencing is mystical or metaphysical and not psychotic, and therefore doesn't warrant clinical or pharmaceutical intervention. But even if it's their own subconscious mechanism leading them to make better choices and feel happier, that's not really something you want to suppress with pills, is it?

As a final note on this topic I want to point out that medical and psychological professionals consider audio and visual hallucinations accepted and even expected phenomena during states such as drunkenness (or detox), extreme tiredness, grieving a loved one's passing, heatstroke, fasting, sensory deprivation, and the moments between being fully awake and fully asleep. While I am not suggesting that psychic ability is actually just hallucination, I wanted to make the point that even hallucinations themselves are not outside the range of normal brain functioning under a wide variety of conditions experienced by relatively healthy people.

The key factor: "Danger to self or others"

Is any of what they're hearing or seeing dangerous to themselves or others? Not just "does it make you uncomfortable?" but are they actually being told to do something to hurt themselves or others? (This is the criterion used by mandated reporters in hospitals, schools, etc.) "Danger to self or others" is a red flag and in such a case, do involve medical and mental health professionals immediately to make sure the situation is managed.

Conversely, even if your loved one is having premonitions about negative stuff, that doesn't necessarily require intervention. If what they see or hear is about a dangerous situation, like an impending catastrophe or a violent crime committed by someone else, that doesn't mean they have a diagnosable mental illness. That's just a common type of precognition (one that most psychics would rather do without).

If your significant other has these kinds of visions, try to keep them from doing something rash like calling news stations to share their predictions of doom and gloom. That might just trigger a snowball of undesired effects.

There are other ways that spirits and other entities can negatively influence a person's life and thought process, as well, but these issues don't respond to mental health protocols anyway so a diagnosis would still not be helpful. (See Chapter 5 to hear how this has affected Brett.)

Remember: "Danger to self or others" is your key to take action and get help immediately.

Even the fact that a person feels crazy doesn't mean they are

I think this statement is pretty self-explanatory so I won't beat you over the head about it, but it is almost inevitable that the person who is experiencing this metaphysical growth will sometimes feel crazy. Especially if their blossoming psychic ability is forcing them to expand their worldview to accept things they previously deemed impossible.

The truth is that despite his lifetime of experience with the esoteric, Brett used to say to me, "I'm not crazy!" periodically in the early days, when telling me about some new information that was triggering his next existential crisis. I always reminded him that I never said nor did I think he was crazy, and he always admitted he was mostly trying to reassure himself.

Periods of growth are typically disorienting and this situation is often that to an extreme degree. Your partner may break down crying or start ranting seemingly out of nowhere from feeling overwhelmed or confused or out of control. Or they may isolate more often or become suddenly fixated on some distracting activity like housework, home improvement projects, working out, shopping, crafts, or watching sports. This still doesn't make them crazy, they're just releasing stress. Support them with empathy and understanding. This too shall pass.

Occasionally people are lying

Of course there's the small chance that a person wants so badly to be psychic that they consciously or unconsciously make up "psychic hits" to satisfy this desire. But this behavior also does not qualify them as mentally ill any more than it would a girl who wrongfully believes she's a good dancer simply because she wishes to be one. Such people may be foolish, but they're not schizophrenic.

Believe it or not, I haven't really run across many people who lie about their psychic ability. Average people, that is. I'm not making any claims about the quality of service you'll receive from your local $5 palm reader, though some storefront psychics are amazingly gifted in addition to knowing how to empty your wallet.

These days, almost every ordinary adult I talk to has a story about "my departed grandmother comes to visit me" or "my wife can see auras" or "I always know right before my brother is going to call." Minor psychic abilities like these are more common than most people realize. Sometimes people don't think to bring it up because it just seems normal to them, but other times I can tell they've been eager for a chance to tell someone.

In any case, it's usually all plausible and credible. Even on occasions when someone shares a type of experience that I don't already know about, I give them the benefit of the doubt as long as I know them to be a generally stable, honest person.

So if your partner is a generally stable, honest person, I encourage you to accept what they are telling you as a genuine accounting of their experience and perception. Even if what they are saying contradicts what you currently believe. That level of trust is essential.

For now, set aside your doubts about the details and focus on your faith in the person. It doesn't mean you're accepting everything they say as a new hard-and-fast rule, only that you're willing to ride shotgun with them on this trip to figure out what is actually true.

So much of reality is subjective

Here are two great quotes about the nature of what we humans like to call "reality."

The question is not what you look at, but what you see.
– Henry David Thoreau

The problem is not the problem. The problem is your attitude about the problem.   – Captain Jack Sparrow

Perception is probably the most important determiner of how we experience the world. We can decide to be happy, satisfied, and grateful, or we can just as easily choose the opposite for ourselves. Either way, our life is mostly going to show up how we expect it to.

One of my best friends had an outdoor wedding. It rained that morning, about which she was distraught because it made the ground muddy and the chairs had to be wiped off. But by the time the guests arrived the air was fresh and clean, and there was a rainbow in all of her wedding photos. It's entirely up to her which way she chooses to spin that story.

In terms of accepting a loved one's development of psychic abilities, consciously choosing to have a positive outlook is going to make everyone's transition to a new normal so much easier. Instead of scary or confusing, try to look at the situation as interesting, exciting, or even fun. Each of these adjectives can be perfectly true, based on your personal decision to think they are.

You may doubt the power of perception to shape our experience of the world, but consider how even situations that are generally agreed upon as problematic are still viewed differently by different people and they would make choices or decisions accordingly. For example, in response to the idea that someone has a major substance-abuse problem, just within my own family I could find people who hold the following beliefs:

- Just needs to try harder to get sober
- Person is deviant and needs to find God or be put in jail
- Should try prescription drugs to ween off the street drugs
- Needs to go to rehab

You can find support in academic literature and popular opinion for all of these responses and yet, they are all entirely based on what one *thinks about* the issue. The case study or data set remains the same, but different people draw different conclusions, leading to a wide range of (often incompatible) suggestions for how to solve the same problem.

As easy as A-B-C

Rational Emotive Behavior Therapy (REBT), one of my two favorite of the non-spiritual counseling approaches, is based on this premise of perception as determiner of response to stimuli.

REBT can literally be simplified to A-B-C, which stands for Activating event-Beliefs-Consequences. That basically means (A) something happens, (B) you have an idea about it—was it good? was it bad?—and then (C) you have a reaction.

The dog steals your sandwich while you're not looking—funny or infuriating? Seeing a ghost—exciting or terrifying? Thunderstorms—charming or disturbing? Based on your beliefs about the meanings of each of these experiences, you will have corresponding emotional responses to them.

The point is that emotional reactions to events are not universal or predetermined. They are based on your thought process, not the other way around.

Let me say that again. *Your emotions do not create your thoughts, your thoughts create your emotions.*

Imagine a grocery store clerk is rude to a customer. There are many different reactions that customer might have, all based on what instantaneous thought happens between the event and the reaction.

One could feel sorry for the clerk because they believe a person must be having a bad day to act like that. Therefore they feel sympathy. Another option is to think a clerk shouldn't dare talk to a customer that way, in which case they'd end up feeling angry. Another is to be completely unconcerned about how a stranger is acting and have no emotional response whatsoever.

None of these reactions are inherently correct; they're all just based on the B in the ABC—the Belief of the beholder. Obviously the people who feel compassion or nothing at all are making the better choices for their own well-being, but these beliefs are so ingrained and subconscious that the angry person sometimes doesn't even realize they have the choice to not get angry.

However, I assure you that a reaction like anger is based on our thought choices and we can change our reactions simply by changing our minds. (But even when something is "simple," I know that doesn't necessarily make it "easy.")

Being angry has no impact on a situation unless you are moved to direct action anyway, so it's a waste of time and energy. The fact that I'm mad that someone took the parking spot I wanted doesn't get me the parking spot, and has no effect on them whatsoever, unless I confront them. And if I do approach them about it, I just look like an out-of-control jerk and I most likely still won't "win" by getting the parking spot.

Considering that most reactions are just based on perspective, you can see why when a loved one is exhibiting non-dangerous traits (even ones you don't like or understand), it is most likely just your thoughts on the subject (in terms of acceptance) that need to change.

If you insist on pursuing a mental health approach to this situation, remember that a diagnosis can stay on a person's record permanently, which would affect their treatment by doctors and insurance companies, potentially for the rest of their lives. In rare cases where one's health background is a consideration for employment, it almost certainly precludes one from getting hired. And taking unneeded medications can cause even more devastating consequences.

These are worst-case scenarios but they happen to people all the time. Does what's happening around your house really warrant that severe of a reaction?

When you have a hammer, everything looks like a nail

Despite all of this, you may still feel that doctors of the psychiatric ilk are authorities and should be the final determiners of whether each person's internal experience (perception) or external experience (behavior) falls within the "normal" range. In response to that I will point out that there are many books written on the fallibility of the *DSM* and our psychiatric diagnosis system, some even by disillusioned psychiatrists who have had the privilege of sitting on a *DSM* committee.

Two of my favorites are *They Say You're Crazy* by Paula J. Caplan, Ph.D. and *The Book of WOE* by Gary Greenberg.

A few common themes raised by those taking a critical stance against the current model of mental health diagnosis include:

- The fact that mental illnesses are diagnosed strictly through interpretation of behaviors. There is no blood test or brain-scan protocol for diagnosing schizophrenia in individuals. The psychiatrist's discretion is the sole determining factor in whether a patient meets the *DSM* criteria for a schizophrenia diagnosis. (The discovery of a genetic biomarker that correlates to a statistically higher vulnerability to schizophrenia is not viewed by the scientific and psychiatric communities as an indicator of actually having schizophrenia, only a heightened chance of developing it—usually during adolescence—if other factors also come into play.)
- As society changes, "mental illnesses" are moved into or out of the *DSM* to reflect the general population's feeling about whether said behavioral patterns are more or less acceptable. (Greenberg uses homosexuality as one example, which was included in the *DSM* until the 1970s and was prior to that sometimes treated with shock therapy. He makes another example of drapetomania, which was the medical/psychiatric name for the alleged mental illness that caused slaves to want to run away from their owners in the 19th century.)
- Even with an agreed-upon diagnosis, psychiatrists use the trial-and-error method with psychopharmaceuticals to figure out what will suppress symptoms in each particular patient. Side effects are many, and the best-case scenario is to modify a patient's behavior through perpetual medication—not through achieving an actual cure of the perceived problem.

Fortunately, many professionals are exploring the issue from other angles, such as Dr. Francis Lu of UC Davis. His 300-page *Religious and Spiritual Issues in Psychiatric Diagnosis* focuses on the differences between what he calls "spiritual conditions" and "psychiatric conditions." But an article he co-authored for publication in the *Psychiatric Annals* in March of 2006 explains my point in just three sentences:

> *Overall, studies have found little relationship between anomalous experiences and psychopathology. Indeed, many of these experiences have been associated with claims of positive life changes after the experience. The majority of these experiences do not cause disruption in psychological, social, or occupational functioning and do not involve mental health treatment.*

There are even classes at some psychology grad schools whose course descriptions emphasize "acknowledging distressing religious and spiritual experiences as non-pathological problems," and some models of psychological thought are based entirely on this premise.

Accept, Accommodate, Adjust

In light of all of these facts, I hope you see now that it is critical to give due consideration before pursuing a mental health approach to your loved one's apparent psychic ability. When he or she does go in for a check-up, do your best to not unduly influence the doctor's evaluation. And insist that your partner research recommendations before agreeing to any particular treatment.

Unless your loved one is exhibiting dangerous behaviors, the more appropriate alternative in most cases is to realize that this change is just another new thing in your life that you can best manage by accepting, accommodating, and adjusting to. Together.

Chapter 5

KEEPING THEM ATTACHED TO THIS VERSION OF REALITY

One of the most essential things you need to do for both of your sakes is make sure your partner remembers how to function in the everyday world, regardless of what kinds of abilities are emerging. You need to help them understand that what is happening is an augmentation of their everyday existence, not a replacement of it. Even Brett's Spirit Guides reiterate this to him periodically, perhaps because it's so easy for him to get singularly focused on the metaphysical.

However, this does not mean that you need to get your partner to forsake or deny what is happening to them or stop doing it, whatever "it" is. It simply means that it is entirely possible for them to incorporate these new abilities and traits into a rich and thoroughly functional everyday life. But they'll likely need your support and assistance to get there.

Unless you've watched someone else navigate this specific life change, you might feel like you are the only couple in the world going through all of this right now. But that's just not true. Many people are experiencing this type of growth and many more have survived and even thrived in similar circumstances in recent history.

Almost everywhere we go, when we are bold enough to raise the topic of psychic development, someone in the room is eager to tell us that it's happening to them or a loved one, too. So don't worry, things will most likely turn out OK if you keep your head on straight and follow some guidelines.

Remember: Psychics are regular people who can do cool stuff

When people's skills are first developing, it can sometimes cause them to become grandiose, expecting others to suddenly revere them like superheroes. And I get it. These abilities are so outside the range of what we consider normal, how could one not feel superior when able to heal with their hands, speak to the dead, or know outcomes before they happen? So of course someone who can do these things might feel pretty special.

Or to the contrary, they may become almost paralyzed because what they're seeing or feeling is scaring them and/or shattering their worldview and they don't know how to respond.

Either extreme can put you in a difficult position as their partner, but their reactions are understandable because what they are experiencing is not something frequently discussed in most segments of our society yet. They probably don't have a point of reference for how to flourish or even cope with this situation.

This can lead to dysfunction that comes in many forms: acting arrogantly, pushing people away, or making rash or bizarre decisions, for example. Some new psychics don't exhibit any significant behaviors besides just wanting more time alone, and that makes it so much easier on those of us who support them. But most of them get a little erratic every once in a while until they've integrated their abilities and developed the necessary humility to realize a very important fact: that they're still a relatively normal person, just one who can do some cool stuff.

Your best move when overinflated or deflated ego is involved is to not overreact. It's a short-term thing. They'll come back toward center naturally if you're supportive but don't get sucked into their drama.

It's sort of like dealing with a teenager, to be honest. You don't want to be dismissive of how they're relating to life but you also don't need to engage at their level of intensity (either in argument or in sympathy) because that just escalates the situation.

During the short period that I had to manage this with Brett (which now thankfully seems so long ago), every discussion we had on the topic was carefully measured and sometimes even pre-planned. As you already know, when you have to talk a person into or out of something, being confrontational usually backfires. So I had to be careful about how I presented my positions.

This approach was largely for my own benefit but also his. The new psychic you love so much is probably already having an internal struggle, perhaps to an even greater extent than they can or will articulate to you. They don't need to be struggling with you, too.

Fortunately, the most important thing you can do to help them (and yourself) is also one of the simplest: Just be supportive of them, wherever they are in their process. It will speed up their adjustment. By helping them feel as OK as possible, you will bring down the stress level in the house. Less turmoil for them means less turmoil for you. Everybody wins.

But I'll reiterate that "simple" isn't always the same as "easy" so don't be too hard on yourself while you're figuring it out day to day.

If I had it to do over again, I think I would handle it more gracefully. "Hindsight is 20/20" and all that. Even relatively mild comments like, "I want you to consider that you might not have all of the information yet" were not particularly well received back then because he couldn't tolerate any bit of judgment from me. He was on one hand feeling almost drunk with the powers that manifested in him abruptly, but at the same time feeling extremely vulnerable because he was questioning his own sanity.

I made the best of the situation by keeping my goals in mind: I wanted Brett to be fully present in our life together again, and I wanted him to be happy. So I finally figured out the best way to do that was to make sure it never seemed like I was dismissing or discounting his perspective.

I'm not saying it's easy to bite your tongue, just that things will work out better if you censor yourself when you can't figure out how to be positive or at least productive. I even have training as a therapist and sometimes the best I could muster was not saying anything at all. He still snaps at me for "therapizing" him when I occasionally listen with a therapist's

"I'm filtering all of my thoughts and opinions" look on my face. But I guarantee that issues get resolved quicker because I maintain my composure.

Prioritize emotional regulation over the content of thought

On the other hand, when he gets especially upset, the most useful strategy is for me to help him regulate his emotional state.

I've learned over the years that I don't need to dwell on the exact words he's saying when he's upset because he'll gain clarity later, either through obtaining more information or just being able process the situation better once he's calmed down. What he really needs is my help getting to that calmer place.

He still gets worked up occasionally when he's reviewing audio recordings to hear messages from spirits or to help validate his impressions of paranormal activity at a site. These recordings are called EVPs (electronic voice phenomena). You may have heard of EVPs and maybe you've dismissed them as nonsense, but I can tell you that though they are inexplicable, they are definitely real.

On the recordings I can hear what we refer to as "audibles" but Brett can hear voices and noises on several levels beyond that. It's different for everyone and it doesn't seem to be based on quality of physical hearing, so we don't have an explanation at this time. Some of our close friends (non-psychics, if there is such a thing) can hear only what I can hear while others can hear more, though not quite as much as Brett. It's kind of mysterious.

But back to my point. Sometimes when he's listening to EVPs he is rattled profoundly. He starts questioning things both practically and philosophically. To be honest, he occasionally makes me nervous with the depth of his distress, but at least I've figured out it's the distress I need to deal with and not the content of what he's saying.

It helps to reassure him that I trust he'll figure it out. That everything is going to be fine. That things have been rough before but they turn out OK. That I'm going to be in it with him even when circumstances seem bleak. And that I believe him, meaning that I believe he heard what he's sure he heard, even if I don't necessarily agree with his initial interpretation of it (but I usually leave that part out in the moment).

You, however, are the expert on your partner, not me. So I know you'll figure out what they specifically need to hear when they've been shaken up by something new and extraordinary.

After he's settled down, he's then able to deal with the information in a calm and level-headed way. Which is always a relief. But since I benefit from his growth process because it lifts me up with him, I suppose being his support when he's shaky is a small price to pay for this amazing life we're living now.

Keep them connected to what has always been important

One way to help our partners stay present and minimize the detrimental effects of ego inflation, self-doubt, or fear is to help them maintain focus on the positive, foundational elements that have defined their lives so far. That would be the kids, us, their jobs, hobbies, friends, volunteering, working out. Whatever is important to them.

Encourage your significant other to still spend time and give priority to these parts of their life, even if they'd rather not. It might be hard to convince them at first because their world seems to be morphing and/or because whatever is happening in their mind is too distracting, but these things are still as important as ever and are also very grounding. (See Chapter 6 for more about grounding.)

Brett loves long rides on his motorcycle. (I mean like Los Angeles-to-the Arctic Circle long.) I prod him to go out whenever he gets the urge because the act of riding is essentially meditative since he has to focus just on the road. And it's not only stress relief. It creates an opportunity for him to navigate new situations, which he finds stimulating and consequently, improves his mood.

Other people get similar beneficial effects from surfing, camping, or practicing an instrument, for example. If he or she prefers activities that are more familiar yet still uplifting, playing with children and having dinner with friends are great ways to maintain healthy connections.

Regardless of what they're interested in, your loved one needs to stay involved in these activities. Despite the amazing changes that are happening within them, don't doubt that they are still here with the primary purpose of living a regular human existence (like the rest of us). Psychic abilities and paranormal experiences should merely be integrated into one's previously established, multi-faceted life.

Hopefully, after their initial disorientation, your partner will be able to redirect most of their attention and energy back to their regular routine, not only of responsibility but also of enjoying and appreciating the things that have always made them happy.

Expect that some of their priorities or preferences might change gradually as a result of being exposed to new information and ways of thinking, though. This is to be expected in any learning/growing situation, of course. But in the beginning, help them maintain focus on whatever has provided structure and meaning up to that point because it's a bad idea to make big decisions or changes when we're feeling emotional or not like ourselves. This is why I promote a "two-week rule." After a significant event, you're not allowed to make any major life decisions (positive or negative) for at least two weeks. Think about how unfocused you are upon coming back from a marvelous vacation, or when you've experienced a break-up or loss. Radical ideas seem reasonable when we're in that state.

Quit your job and move to Hawaii? Sure, why not? Life was like one big party while you were there, right? What could possibly go wrong? But two weeks or a month later you'll realize that upending your whole life overnight that way probably isn't the best decision.

The same applies to making important decisions or changes soon after one's psychic ability surfaces. There's too much emotion and uncertainty to be a smart decision maker at that point. Try to help your partner slow down if they want to veer off onto a different path while they're still disoriented.

Get clear about the lifestyle of modern-day mystics

Our culture has romanticized concepts of monks sitting in mountaintop caves pondering philosophy and prophets wandering the Earth barefoot, but these are not the paths of the modern-day mystic. Continuing to participate in our communities with an elevated perspective is how we can best be of service in this era. Not to mention being the only way to survive.

These days, you need money if you hope to have food and clothes and other extravagances like transportation and a decent place to live. And on average we prefer people to have some kind of independent income to provide for their own needs instead of relying solely on the generosity of others. Even if someone is contributing in an abstract way, rather than in a way that adheres to societal norms, they are sometimes still considered a slacker or burden.

Consequently, the ancient models of mysticism don't work anymore.

Of all the psychics and healers we count among our friends and colleagues, only one of them is thoroughly preoccupied with her metaphysical work to the exclusion of many other aspects of her life. She's single, her son is grown, and she has decided to acquiesce to the 24/7 flow of deceased people trying to contact the living through her. She works with clients almost all day, every day, and into the night. She's doing amazing work but it takes a huge toll on her. At least she still goes to the gym every day, which has always been important to her.

The rest of the working psychics and healers we know either do their spiritual work as a second job, or only on rare occasion (perhaps on a *pro bono* basis), or they have a practice with reasonable business hours so they can still be involved with family and unrelated interests. Others have found that teaching or writing is the best way to use their skills to make a living.

In other words, the new standard is to incorporate metaphysical work into an otherwise normal life.

For the first few months Brett did have a hard time accepting that the mundane aspects of life should still be important to him. I don't mean family and pets, of course. I mean having a job, taking care of household responsibilities, banking, etc. Things that at first consideration seemed anathema to the fantastical, spiritual journey upon which he had embarked. Things that seemed contrary to the romanticized image of mysticism.

He had to get to the point where he could remember that paying bills is still necessary. That he's here as a human being to do all the things a person does, only he happens to be a person who is also a medium and channel, a person who is also a healer. That he wasn't being given gifts so he could drop out of society, spending his days focused on the spirit world and tuned out of the "real" world. He was being given gifts to share with as many people as possible, and he could only do that by engaging with his surroundings in a functional and socially acceptable way, using the tools and methods that connect people today.

It didn't take too long for us, fortunately. Soon his ability to maintain balance between family, work, and practice was back to normal and life began functioning as smoothly as before. To be honest, many aspects of our lives are actually better. Feeling more fulfilled from his enhanced connection with a Higher Power and the way he is able to help people has led to him feeling happier and positive more of the time.

But it wasn't something I could just tell him to do or force him into. I couldn't push him farther or faster than he was ready to go, regardless of my own discomfort level. We all know how counterproductive it is to push someone too hard. They fight back instinctively and any future progress comes at an even higher price.

So I just supported him through the rough patch in the beginning, making subtle suggestions when appropriate. Eventually, knowing that he could still count on me helped him find his own stability. Gradually he was able to start seeing with a clearer mind. Then calm, rational discussions about the lifestyle of modern-day mystics arose and we were able to frame the subject of his growth and transition as a team project that we would confidently manage together.

Recognize and redirect any temptation to self-medicate

Something that happens quite frequently, unfortunately, is that people who are beginning their psychic awakening turn to substances to numb themselves out because they're scared. Having abilities emerge can be uncomfortable, especially if you feel alone or when it seems like there's not much support in the general community (which may or may not be true, depending on where you live). So the answer, again, is that they'll be looking to you to be that support they need so much.

Some psychic abilities do actually cause scary or distressing images, sensations, or knowledge. For example, your significant other might periodically be able to predict impending tragedies yet have no way to warn anyone. Or if they're empathic they might feel the pain, illness, sadness, and fear of another as if it was their own. Even when they know it's coming from someone else it can still be uncomfortable.

A common example of self-medicating is when someone is disturbed by hearing voices or seeing things move around at night so they start smoking marijuana when they didn't used to or taking excessive amounts of over-the-counter pills to get to sleep. Short-term solutions that cause long-term problems.

Intoxication, whether it be with alcohol or drugs (prescribed or otherwise), can interfere with psychic ability (and in many cases, common sense). This is why it's such a common method people use to "turn off" their abilities when they're not ready to embrace them. Of course there are drugs that expand one's perception rather than shut it down, but people generally don't use them to escape because they have the opposite effect.

Now I won't get into the purported physical benefits or detriments of any particular substance, but I will say that being under the influence changes your vibration. Consequently, drugs and alcohol can make a person even more vulnerable to other-dimensional energies. In the same way that shutting your eyes doesn't actually make anything go away, masking your psychic sensitivity through substance use doesn't change what's hanging around, only your ability to perceive and respond to it. So just be sure your significant other is making an informed decision, not an impulsive one.

Sure, most of us have vices or at least bad habits. We're all imperfect and no one should expect otherwise. But the red flag is an *increase* in alcohol consumption, cigarette smoking, or even eating junk food, which could be signs that your partner is using those mechanisms to deal with stress.

If you notice a change, be cautious in how you approach the situation. Focusing chiefly on a problem behavior often just causes a rift between loved ones and eliminates opportunities to address the real issue. Instead, deal with the cause (stress? fear? confusion?), not the symptom. Help them process the underlying emotion in order to return to their usual, healthier patterns.

Be especially careful if someone already has a proclivity toward substance abuse or escaping difficult situations by numbing themselves out. Having a very supportive person in their life, and that means you, can go a long way toward fending off the impulse to use that crutch during spiritual growth.

This is not to say, of course, that a person currently struggling with addiction can just be talked out of it. I have too much personal and professional experience with that to be so naïve. No, I'm referring here to someone who is not currently using substances to self-medicate but who would be tempted to try it because of the extreme discomfort they're experiencing. That behavior can spiral out of control quickly so be vigilant and address the issue as soon as possible.

Make sure their issues are really their issues

Since we're talking about addiction, I want to point out other ways a psychic can be impacted by substance-related issues.

Brett had an interesting paranormal experience that was not at all his fault but which still impacted him greatly and required decisive action. He became "attached" by a spirit who had had a drinking problem. ("Attachments" are ghosts who try to ride along in a human's energy field so they can vicariously re-experience something they miss from being alive. Usually attachments bring undesirable traits to their hosts such as anger, depression, violence, addiction, etc.)

As a result, Brett started exhibiting alcoholic behaviors. He was drinking every day, which was severely out of character for him. His agitated rationalization was that "he deserved it" or "it would take the edge off." He would get angry when I suggested he was drinking too much. This hostility had no precedent in our relationship.

Fortunately, he was already well-versed in the kinds of effects that other dimensions can have upon us, so after about two weeks, when he caught himself pouring a drink before work, he realized he was being influenced by an external source. He was able to identify and evict the attachment and immediately felt his drive to drink evaporate, though he remembers how strong the compulsion can be and treats alcohol differently than he did before this incident.

This incident led to his increased interest in removing attachments from other people in order to eliminate unnatural outside influences. Of course we all have our issues that we need to work on, but we don't have to tolerate other spirits putting their issues on us, too.

Detecting and removing attachments is a sort of specialization within the psychic/healing field, so if you think someone you love is being unduly influenced by a spirit hanger-on, please seek the help of an experienced practitioner. (It can happen to anyone.)

Another reason your psychic partner may be feeling the need for a drink or smoke is if they're highly empathic and spend lots of time around someone else who is having these cravings. I know sensitive people, usually younger people, who haven't figured out how to protect themselves yet so they find it almost impossible to regulate their own emotions. They feel whatever someone else near them is feeling instead of having the boundaries and distinct sense of self that most of us have. It can be highly disruptive.

If your newly psychic loved one is experiencing these kinds of cravings, be sure to give adequate consideration to these possibilities. Is it their problem or someone else's? The information in the next chapter on grounding and protection will be extra useful for them if this is the case.

Reconcile old and new beliefs

If the abilities your partner is demonstrating are upsetting the balance in your household, one likely reason is that they might fall outside of the parameters of your current spiritual belief system. In that case (which is most people's cases), you'll have to be willing to expand the bubble of what you consider "real" in order to keep life from flying apart at the seams.

You might think, "Well, that's easy for you to say!" But trust me, I've had to go through continuous shifts and expansions of my worldview due to Brett's ever-growing repertoire, and I'm 100% sure we're not done yet.

Remember, I was raised non-religious. In my youth I thought the Bible and all other religious texts were merely stories created by well-intentioned men; allegories to teach lessons based on historical perspectives. The same with so-called myths, aboriginal creation stories, and so on.

And despite the fact that we're radically open-minded people, there are still days that force us to embrace the existence of some fantastical, other-dimensional entity that we previously didn't believe in. It's funny that Brett's favorite quote has always been Shakespeare's "There are more things in heaven and earth, Horatio, than are dreamt of in your philosophy." I certainly didn't know how true that was until all of these accelerated changes started happening for him.

Reconciling new experience with existing spiritual beliefs may be the hardest part of the process for some. Religious teachings are often considered inviolable, indisputable. That's why it's essential to find the ways in which these phenomena fit within your current framework to the greatest extent possible to try to minimize this internal conflict.

Perhaps you're concerned that psychic activity is heretical, blasphemous, or evil. If the idea is completely outside of your range of experience, I can see how such questions might arise. You might be able to point to scriptures that warn against it to support that perspective.

However, I've been assured by people better studied than myself that there are an equal number of passages, if not more, that explicitly promote the phenomenon as a positive, naturally occurring part of our human experience.

And while I claim expertise in no particular religion, from my own studies I know that pretty much every denomination and belief system has mysticism in its history and makes room for direct experiencing of the Divine.

Which is what most psychics will tell you is exactly what's happening to them during practice—connecting with the Divine.

A good example is that healers almost always say they aren't healing anyone but that healing is happening *through* them, and the ability comes from a Higher Power.

The heightened connection to "All" that psychics usually feel often inspires them to live more conscientious lives, so from a practical standpoint, the development and use of psychic abilities bears out positive results most of the time. It brings beneficial outcomes to individuals and communities and incrementally moves society toward higher consciousness.

Like when a medium gives a message to a client or stranger, the content is usually of a loving nature from the other side. Psychic investigators use their abilities to give police detectives critical pieces of information so they can find kidnapping victims and perpetrators of violent crimes. Pet psychics help remedy behavior problems that might otherwise land a vulnerable dog or cat in the local shelter.

Could there possibly be a better functional expression of the core precepts of all spiritual traditions from around the world or the idea of "The Golden Rule?"

I propose that perhaps the truly hard part isn't accepting that psychic phenomena are OK and are happening in the world, just that they're happening to us personally. They seem so magical and otherworldly.

So let's get one thing straight—yes, your partner is worthy. And you are worthy. Really take that in. All you have to do is change your mind and you will change your life, almost certainly for the better. Help your significant other internalize this idea, too.

Cultivate gratitude

One of Brett's psychic advisors one time said to me (in front of him), "I have a message from one of his Spirit Guides." The message was: *Gratitude will keep him safe.*

This instantly made a lot of sense to us. And I think it probably applies to everyone.

Gratitude makes us feel better because we're in the mindset of thankfulness instead of a mindset of lack or entitlement. This concept is recognized universally now. The magazine *Psychology Today* explains, "Studies show that we can deliberately cultivate gratitude and can increase our well-being and happiness by doing so."

Gratitude for what's going right helps us keep from taking things for granted. It helps us maintain our focus on the bigger picture of what's really important. It definitely guards against excessive ego or narcissism because if one is thankful, that perspective draws the person away from the conclusion that they are inherently superior.

That's not to say there aren't lots of rewards we each deserve due to merit. But gratitude allows us to keep from being arrogant about those achievements. It keeps us humble.

My own first foray into gratitude as an intentional state of mind was working through *Simple Abundance* by Sarah Ban Brethnach some 20 years ago. At the time her suggestion to list things for which I was grateful each and every day, even when I had to push really hard to come up with something, seemed revolutionary to me. Now gratitude is such a staple of self-help rhetoric that I question whether I was the only one in the world who hadn't figured it out back then.

That book changed my life in many ways, all for the good, using gratitude as a foundational mechanism to recreate myself. So when we got the message "gratitude will keep him safe," it felt familiar and right. Brett interpreted it as needing to be thankful especially for the gifts he was exhibiting, the beings who were helping him, and the experiences he'd been blessed with. This has worked out very well in helping keep him grounded and positive.

And when it feels like life is getting tough—metaphysically, physically, or financially—we return to the feeling of gratitude for everything that is going right instead of focusing on what we lack, and we realize that our lives are actually pretty fantastic (in both meanings of the word).

Encourage them to meditate (and you should do it, too)

Since we're on the subject of keeping our heads on straight, let's talk about the value of meditation.

It has been widely demonstrated that everyone can benefit from meditation. For a person with emerging psychic abilities, in addition to the typical benefits of decreased anxiety and increased clarity of thought, meditation will most likely also have the effect of strengthening and speeding up their acquisition of skills. When he's helping people develop their skills, Brett always places a lot of emphasis on the importance of meditation because it helps connect us with our Higher Selves and beyond.

But aside from that, studies show that people who meditate regularly are better able to *respond* to situations instead of just *reacting* to them. Increased self-control is considered a desirable skill for all people in all areas of life. So even if you're not seeking out methods for them to enhance their abilities at this point, you can see how the standard physiological and cognitive effects of meditation—calming them down and helping them think more clearly—would be to everyone's benefit. (Meaning your own sanity as well as theirs.)

There are so many approaches and schools of thought on meditation that I will just encourage you to do your own research and find what works for each of you. Or for both of you, together.

I've heard that some couples find sitting together for meditation to be deeply bonding, leading to greater intimacy. In fact, there are forms of tandem meditation designed specifically for this purpose. I personally find it more difficult because having Brett in the room is just one more potential distraction. It's hard enough to get three small dogs settled down adequately for me to concentrate. But it's a completely personal preference that warrants experimentation and consideration.

Just so I'm being completely honest, this is the piece of my own advice that I don't follow as well as I should. I only meditate a few times per week and originally I could only focus for maybe two minutes at a time without becoming extremely distracted. My mind would go so far off track that several minutes later I'd remember that I was supposed to be meditating but I had started doing something else entirely. I'd even find myself looking at my phone, momentarily oblivious to why I'd been sitting on the bed in the first place.

Now I can easily meditate for 15 minutes or sometimes a little longer. It helps to use an app that chimes at my desired intervals, which removes a major preoccupation that used to interfere with my mindfulness—the question of how long I'd been sitting.

Monitoring the in and out of my breath works sometimes but other times, it's not a rich enough focus to keep my attention. That's why I sometimes use imagery like breathing in colors or seeing oxygen flow to parts of my body where I need healing. Or really, whatever else can keep my mind calmly focused because the old suggestion of trying to not think of anything at all just doesn't work for me.

Experiment with different techniques for yourself and perhaps more importantly, encourage your significant other to figure out how to meditate on a regular basis if they don't already. And don't be intimidated by old-school ideas about the seriousness and difficulty of meditation. It's not "all that." You can each figure out a version that works for you and that's fine.

Both of you should keep a journal

On top of everything else you have to do, keeping a journal seems really, really low on the priority list, I understand. I used to think Brett was being kind of silly insisting on writing in it every day so I didn't start doing it as soon as he did.

But after a while we started coming up with different opinions about what happened when, and I realized that while I felt like I could remember all the details, having my version written down on a regular basis helped ensure we had a more complete and accurate picture of the way things were developing.

I didn't write in a diary as a girl and I've only recently been consistent in keeping my appointments on the calendar in my phone. For some reason I'm resistant to these kinds of routines. However, I write in my journal almost every day now because it's just that important.

Mine's not a "what I had for lunch" journal, although you can write whatever you want in yours. I write almost exclusively about our paranormal/spiritual/metaphysical experiences. As crazy as this sounds, considering the subject matter, our journals are actually like the kinds of notes scientists might take during an experiment. Data, observations, hypotheses. But yours can be whatever you want it to be and your partner's might be something different.

In combination our journals help us track trends and growth as well as the beginnings and endings of certain phenomena. They give us a record of the exact time and date when particularly noteworthy stuff happened. They also show our fluctuations in attitude toward what's going on.

As more outrageous stuff happens, the stuff we used to think was extreme now seems commonplace. I remember when we figured out there was the spirit of a teenage boy hiding in the corner of our kitchen by the refrigerator. (Where else would a teenage boy hang out besides by the fridge?). He'd been there for years and was probably the cause of the apprehension I often felt when letting the dogs out at night.

It seemed like a big deal at the time. Now we realize there are multiple spirits passing through and hanging out here basically all the time and we don't think twice about it unless they're pestering the dogs. But it's important to have an ongoing record so we can remember where we came from and we're not letting our memories fool us.

Brett has smartly started dictating his notes periodically through speech-to-text software in order to make them searchable but he still writes them initially in little pocket-sized notebooks. (Think Sean Connery's notebook in *Indiana Jones and the Last Crusade*.) Despite my general bent toward functionality and practicality, I prefer the larger ornate journals sold at bookstores for too much money.

It's a really good idea for each of you to get a notebook or journal that you like and start writing notes every day about what has happened and what you think and how you feel about it. For now, maybe you just have to take my word for it, but I can almost guarantee that your accurate, detailed record is going to be indispensable at some point in the future. Get started now.

And then…reach out

I know I've emphasized keeping things close to home and being the prime point of support for your partner, but once you've got a grip on your situation, consider using outside resources to optimize this growth process and help bring your life back to a comfortable balance as quickly as possible.

In some cases, your support will be all they need, but I have to say that most people I know who've gone through this transformation find it helpful or even critical to connect with others on their same path. And since this is where things start to shift out of your jurisdiction, so to speak, I can understand if you become a little nervous about it at first.

As humans we're generally most comfortable when we maintain the sense (or illusion) of control over our lives and relationships so we may get nervous when change is imposed upon us. But your partner's desire to reach out for fellowship is positive and natural in the same way that a child's development of social autonomy is both inevitable and beneficial, even if sometimes bittersweet.

Consequently, part of your research should be helping them find a community of people who can relate to their experiences. You might be pleasantly surprised and find there are actually support options in your neighborhood. But if not, your significant other might have to settle for an online group (or perhaps they would actually prefer that).

Meetup.com is a good place to look for these groups, which are sometimes called "development circles" or may have the words "psychic," "spiritual," "mediumship," "channeling," "metaphysical," or "healing" in the group name, depending on what type of ability your loved one is exhibiting and what lingo is being used in your community by "those people."

There are also websites like spiritualforums.com and psychic-experiences.com, for example, and you can find other options by Googling them.

Just use your reasoning skills and familiar channels to track down whatever best fits your lifestyle. This is simply another project for the two of you to tackle together. It will be a work in progress so keep an open mind and trust that whatever you're supposed to find at any particular time will be available to you. Sort of like that saying "When the student is ready, the teacher will appear" that is often (mis)attributed to Buddha.

We have tried out various groups here in Los Angeles. Some we liked a lot and some we disliked to an equal degree, but never have we considered them a waste of time. These were all just learning opportunities that brought us closer together. Even when only one of us attends, we both end up learning from it since we always share what happened at a meeting or class.

Another way that reaching out has been useful is that we found a professional psychic who Brett now visits periodically for his own readings. Yes, even though he is a psychic himself, he still enjoys getting read by someone else (as long as they're really adept). This woman validates and clarifies a lot of information that he has already picked up from spirit sources, without him telling her about it ahead of time. She lets me sit in on the sessions so I can take notes, which not all psychics allow.

My point is that finding other people with abilities isn't just beneficial because it increases our partners' peace of mind to know they're not alone, but also because they have skills that can actually come in handy. We all like having buddies who can provide professional services and advice (lawyer, doctor, massage therapist?) and this is no different. It's both useful and fun to have psychics and healers in our social circles.

Don't let the green-eyed monster get the best of you

Try not to react to your loved one's impulse to reach out for friendship with jealousy, resentment, vindictiveness, guilt trips, or any other dysfunctional attitude. Of course, with all of the new relationships that will be forming for both of you, it's natural to feel a little jealous about a few of these individuals or about having to share your time and attention.

It makes sense. Prior to this you had an unspoken agreement about the relationship between the two of you, and your relationship between the two of you and the outside world. This situation may have forced both of you to invite and accept new members into the circle of your life, which can always create the potential for jealousy or mistrust.

For people in open and polyamorous relationships, jealousy is less likely to be an issue because the idea of sharing one's partner is already integral to that lifestyle. But most people still choose monogamy when they're really serious about someone, and the sense of stability that comes from exclusivity is sometimes challenged when new players enter the picture.

Therefore, if we imagine a scenario where you are not a supporter, but instead are a detractor or critic of your partner, then you would have legitimate concerns about your loved one needing to seek comfort outside of your relationship. Because they definitely need it, from you or someone else. But since you've decided to be a supportive, actively involved partner, what they'll need from others will be just information, validation, and camaraderie.

Brett has developed friendships and working relationships with several women who are also practicing psychics. One of them is even a ridiculously gorgeous model on top of being a talented medium. But since I've made myself an integral, essential, and positive part of Brett's life, I feel confident that he's interacting appropriately with these women even when I'm not around.

I have also opened up to becoming friends with them myself, much to my own benefit. As you might imagine, they're some of the most interesting characters I've ever met. I now consider many of them to be my personal friends, aside from his relationship with them. In fact, almost all of the people I'd consider new friends in the past 10 years have come from this part of our life. Since finding new friends can be difficult as adults because we're so busy and our routines don't expose us to a lot of candidates, I'm thankful that we've found such a qualified applicant pool.

Sure, there are going to be associates you don't like, but that happens in all areas of life. Work colleagues, an old classmate at a high school reunion, someone who just moved in down the street. But make sure it's due to the fact that they're actually unlikeable and not due to unfounded jealousy. Just be your partner's #1 fan instead and save the wasted energy of playing out a fabricated rivalry.

(All bets are off if your partner has a pattern of infidelity, though. If that's your situation, you have more important things to worry about than whether they're actually psychic or not.)

The truth is, the uniqueness of this situation gives you an advantage—the chance to understand each other and bond in a way that many couples never will. Keep returning to that point when you start to feel annoyed or nervous.

In many ways this situation is not inherently different than any other transitional period you might experience during a relationship. Outside circumstances are forcing change and growth for both of you, and I'm sure that has happened before and you figured out how to overcome it, together. So too you will overcome this.

Chapter 6

GROUNDING AND PROTECTION

In the previous chapter I talked about the importance of helping someone stay focused on their day-to-day life and also about keeping their ego reasonably in check. These are essential strategies for making sure everybody and everything stays on track.

There is also a process called "grounding" that people in the metaphysical world use to keep themselves healthy and safe and it's important enough that I'm dedicating a whole chapter to it.

Though attitude and intention are the most fundamental mechanisms for self-protection and success, it's a good idea for you and your significant other to learn specific energetic grounding and protection techniques because they're relevant for anyone practicing psychic or healing skills, as well as those around them.

I want to say up front that you shouldn't let my mention of self-defense worry you. These are mostly precautionary measures so little things don't turn into big things. Think of using these processes and tools as similar to bolstering one's immune system. Making sure that minor annoyances don't turn into stress-induced illnesses. Or maybe compare it to doing preventive maintenance on your car. It's just more sensible to be proactive and not take unnecessary risks.

We all have Spirit Guides looking out for us so that level of protection is always available, but they generally won't step in unless explicitly asked or if it's an emergency. Humans have free will and must ask for "our team on the other side" to intervene on our behalf or lend us additional support. If you ask, you will usually get the information, guidance, or shielding that you need from them.

But just like we can't expect doctors to fix us if we're not willing to change our habits, we can't expect our Guides to do all the work of protecting us without taking some responsibility for ourselves.

What does grounding even mean?

Energetic grounding is basically the first step in what we consider "psychic protection." It is often taught as the visualization of roots growing from the bottoms of your feet down through the Earth—a metaphor for feeling as steady, earthy, and connected as a tree.

A common protocol goes something like this:

Sit in a comfortable position with your feet on the floor and close your eyes. Take a few deep breaths to bring your awareness into yourself. By focusing on your breathing you can let other thoughts go for now. (This, by the way, is the foundation of meditation. If you can do this, you are meditating!)

Now imagine that there are tree roots growing out of the bottom of your feet and down from your spine. Down into the Earth. As deep as you can make them go. As the roots spread out, imagine that they're pulling you tightly to the Earth, so you're really anchored there.

Take a few moments and a few more deep breaths to really experience yourself as connected to the Earth.

When you're ready, slowly open your eyes.

When someone says to "visualize" or "imagine," don't think that you have to actually see anything in your mind for it to work. Some people have trouble with visuals and instead get a feeling. Or really, just setting your intention to be successful and trusting that it's happening is usually adequate, even if you're not having any sensory response.

This applies in almost all circumstances when someone tells you to visualize something for psychic or metaphysical purposes. Seeing the target in your mind is just one way of engaging with it. Don't get stuck on the word "visualization" and feel like you're doing it wrong if you can't see anything. Just trust. Intention is the key.

There are many techniques similar to the tree roots approach to energetic grounding, all designed to achieve that same sense of solidness. All of the sequences are really quite simple and as I've said, they rely mostly upon intention and visualization (and occasionally a symbolic item, but only if the person so desires).

People (and animals) have inherently different degrees of groundedness. For example, I've been told by psychics that I am exceptionally grounded. One even said it's as if I am "walking ankle deep in the Earth itself." (That's one of my favorite compliments I've ever received.) And I already knew that about myself before anyone else said it. So basically it's like I don't need to ground because I'm a walking ground for others.

Now in comparison, think of someone you consider spacy, whose "head is in the clouds," or who seems like a balloon that might float away if they weren't tethered to something. This type of person is easily identifiable as ungrounded. There are many legitimate reasons for a person to not want to engage thoroughly with our dense reality, but in order for them to achieve genuine balance in their lives, those people need to figure out how to reestablish their energetic bond with the Earth.

However, just because someone you meet has a lofty thought process or a worldview that seems unrealistic to you, that does not necessarily mean they are ungrounded. Consider the Dalai Lama and how he embodies both groundedness and elevation of thought.

Most people fall somewhere in between the two extremes (like with any other characteristic) and our levels are always in flux. So there shouldn't be judgment about anybody's position on the grounded/ungrounded spectrum because we're all just trying to figure out our own optimal functioning and health.

The importance of grounding

When your loved one first exhibits their psychic gifts, even if they were very grounded before, it is likely that they will become somewhat less grounded until they learn how to integrate their new skills into their life. The same kind of diminished groundedness can happen under many ordinary positive and negative circumstances, as well, such as having a baby or being newly in love, or grieving over the loss of a family member or job. This is all natural and you don't have to panic, just make sure you're helping them move in the right direction.

Grounding links our bodies' energy to the Earth's energy so for people who are highly psychically gifted, energetic grounding is absolutely critical because they might leave their bodies frequently, either intentionally or unintentionally. We want them connected here as securely as possible.

Your partner might even do part of their work in different dimensions on purpose. Making sure they're anchored through grounding can keep them from losing touch with reality (or shall we say, crossing over that line from psychic to psychotic) and will help minimize or "ground out" any negative energy that comes back with them. (Think of it as analogous to grounding in electrical systems.)

On a few occasions early on, before he learned to effectively ground, Brett felt like he was spiritually and energetically drifting too far away from this physical dimension while practicing, so he would ask me to grab his hand to shift his course and bring him back to this plane of reality. Based on the extent of his ability to work interdimensionally, he'd been warned to be careful about going too far for too long. So it turns out that the depth of my roots made me the perfect foil to his tendency to float away. As usual, together we are more than the sum of our parts.

Your loved one's need for grounding may not be so extreme or literal, though. They will probably only need to learn techniques like the one I mentioned initially in order to ground their own energy and your role will be mostly as a reminder of home base and as emotional support. You represent the place they want to return to when they've been off in la la land for a little while. If they want your touch during practice it will probably just be for reassurance and comfort.

Grounding techniques are actually good for everyone, though, even people who aren't doing any kind of spiritual or metaphysical work. There's a reason the saying "keeping your feet on the ground" has positive connotations. Being grounded is the first phase of protection from the energetic/psychic negativity and nonsense that's swirling around all of us each and every day. That's why it's worth trying it for yourself.

There are ample suggestions online if you're not satisfied with the tree roots technique. Or if you prefer a guided meditation (where someone walks you through the process via audio recording instead of you having to remember the steps) there are also plenty of options for that format.

Psychic protection

Related to grounding are what we call psychic protection techniques, which you use to protect your energy from the negativity or neediness of others. Psychic protection keeps them from draining you, keeps them from changing your mood based on their issues. Even people who are not practicing psychics benefit greatly from learning this type of self-defense.

You may have heard the term "psychic vampire" or "energy vampire"—the people who suck energy out of you by their mere presence. People who always make you feel bad to be around them, even if they're not saying anything negative. You can ward off such an intentional or unintentional assault with psychic self-defense. (And common sense dictates that we not associate with those people anyway, if we can help it.)

Psychic protection can also help in situations where group energy is overwhelming, which is a very common feeling even for people without psychic sensitivity. Or perhaps more accurately, with unacknowledged psychic sensitivity.

I'm sure you know people who avoid crowded places because it just feels too intense for them. Maybe you're one of those people. Perhaps you've always chalked that up to the noise level or even too much body odor. Indeed, those sensations can be annoying to most of us but they can actually be painful to people with hypersensitivity to sound or smell. (Granted, hypersensitivity is also associated with other physical, cognitive, and psychiatric conditions, but here we're just focusing on psychic sensitivity.)

But many people's vague sense of discomfort when in large groups is due to the fact that their energetic space is being invaded. Think of it as analogous to being overpowered by a terrible smell. It feels like the stench gets on us. It distracts from whatever we were doing. We want to make sure it doesn't stick to us. This is similar to how someone who's sensitive to energy can feel another person's moods. It's distracting. It's invasive. It's uncomfortable. It may be putting them in the bad mood that they've sensed from the other person. They want to avoid that.

Sensitive people having a visceral reaction to being bombarded with emotions might not make sense to those who can't feel others' energy because everything seems fine to them. But the sensitive won't want to go to a concert or sporting event or even the movies, because for them it's like not wanting to hang out at a garbage dump.

However, these people (whether they label their empathy as psychic ability or not) can significantly diminish the discomfort of being around others by employing psychic protection and grounding.

Intention to be protected

As with grounding, most psychic protection techniques are easy, requiring only your imagination/visualization and your intention to be protected. You might be tired of hearing about intention but it is arguably the strongest force at work when talking about the subtler aspects of our existence so I'm going to keep bringing it up.

Someone could do a master's guided meditation for psychic self-protection and if they're going through the motions but also secretly thinking "this isn't going to work," then guess what? They just wasted their time and shouldn't expect any results.

On the other hand, a person who uses no technique at all but is confident that they are protected will have a shift in their energetics that results in them being safer than the naysayer who toiled.

Techniques

Our primary defense against negativity, of course, is to make good choices. Stay away from situations and people that bring you down or give you a bad gut feeling whenever possible. But since that's not always an option, it's valuable to know some psychic protection techniques to help bolster your energetic immune system.

Similar to grounding, most of these techniques utilize visualization. Again, don't get tripped up by thinking you actually have to see anything, even though the term visualization seems to imply that. Imagine, intend, trust that you are being protected through your efforts.

By far, the most common technique is simply surrounding yourself in a ball of white light, with the expectation of being protected by this sphere of energy. (White light is almost universally considered positive and protective, and sometimes healing, so you will hear about it a lot as you learn about psychic and metaphysical techniques.)

As you envision/feel this ball of white energy materialize around you, your heart and mind need to be on board with the process. You need to say to yourself (can be in your head) something to the extent of "I am surrounded and protected by white light. I am only touched by the energy that uplifts me and serves my highest good." And then trust it's going to work. You don't need to be continuously putting energy toward it. Make part of the intention that it will work even when you're not actively thinking about it.

Too easy, right? I told you this stuff was simple. But you need to embrace its power to work for you, not be dismissive because it seems too basic (or too illogical) to be effective. Intention, intention, intention. It works!

Depending on the circumstances, people may add other colors or additional protective imagery or metaphors. The variations are almost endless.

For example, if they feel a strong negative vibe coming at them, they might imagine a bubble or force field that is mirrored on the outside. Then if someone projects negative energy at them, it is merely reflected back. That way they aren't actually being actively negative. In fact, if someone was radiating love to them, the mirror would equally reflect love back, right? This is good because we want to cultivate a mindset of doing no harm, even against those we believe in the moment to be our enemies.

Brett taught one of his eighth-grade students a version of this technique about five years ago. The boy was feeling defeated by what he experienced as relentless browbeating by the girls in his middle school classes. (Can you blame him?) Within a few days he came back and told Brett he was feeling much better—less assaulted, more in control—now that he knew how to activate his shield when the girls were getting intense. How's that for a life skill they don't usually teach you in school?

Be forewarned, though. The downside of the mirrored bubble is that nothing positive gets in either, so it's only for use in situations where you are actively experiencing hostility from someone. You don't want to be cut off from the healthy exchange of energy between you and your surroundings for very long. As our skin needs to breathe, our energy needs to flow.

Extra layering and complicated shielding beyond white light are not necessary for most people or most situations, but some people get pretty elaborate. I would dare say unnecessarily so except that everyone has to do what they believe will work. Go with what makes sense to you instead of copying someone else's protocol just because they claim it works for them. So if swirling ribbons of razor wire are what it's going to take for you to feel protected from a particularly strong negative force in your life, go for it. I personally like to just decide that I am protected and let it be so.

Shields are a good proactive way to keep our energy separate from others' and "cutting cords" is also important. By cords we mean the energetic connections we establish with others when interacting or even just thinking about them. These connections are represented visually (in your mind's eye) by what appear to be actual cords reaching from each person to the other.

Having a lot of cords built up is like having too many devices plugged into one power source. So sometimes, when we feel like someone is having too much influence on us, when we've done psychic/healing practice, or when we just feel drained in general, we need to envision cutting not just the cords between us and one person but between us and everyone.

Don't worry—the ones that are supposed to be there will grow back naturally. You're not going to be disengaged from your closest loved ones. But you will be releasing people and entities who have improperly connected to you and may be taking advantage of your psychic and emotional energy.

Some of these cords manifested a long time ago. So long that you don't even realize those people are still draining or influencing you. Just let all of the cords go and trust that the positive ones will reestablish themselves without any conscious effort on your part.

To do this, just close your eyes and see all cords being cut away or disconnecting from your body. You can imagine using scissors or even a machete if that helps. Whatever instinctively works for you. I use a "quick release" visualization: all of the cords disengage simultaneously and fly away from me as if they're being retracted back to their points of origin.

You can find information about these and myriad other grounding and protection techniques on the internet or in books. There are practically as many techniques as there are teachers so it behooves you to seek out a protocol that feels right for you and not just limit yourself to whatever I've mentioned briefly.

Experiment with them in the privacy of your own comfortable space so you can use them on the spot when you need them. And when your partner is feeling under assault, remind them to put up a shield. When they're feeling unduly influenced by someone, remind them to cut cords. Teamwork!

Tools for protection

Some people use tools, like crystals, for protection. I know several women who wear pendants or bracelets to make sure the specific energetic properties of those stones stay close to their bodies. Some men prefer to keep stones in a pocket but many wear a pendant or bracelet. I've seen men who never wore any jewelry besides a wedding ring who suddenly find comfort and meaning in wearing a bracelet or necklace with stones and religious symbolism of personal significance. You never know what's going to change when psychic ability emerges.

And lots of people (including me, and probably some people you know personally) keep crystals around the house to create an environment of peace and safety in their domain.

While the "encyclopedias" of crystals list the properties of hundreds of stones, there are a few that are most commonly recommended for protection. Quartz, black tourmaline, and the combination of both (tourmalated quartz) are fundamental and are favorites of ours. Now that you have a psychic in the house, you should definitely consider getting some. Hematite and amethyst are usually considered principal stones for protection on most lists, too. Beyond those, you can experiment on your own or get suggestions from websites or your local metaphysical store.

I've tried a wide range of stones favored by psychics I admire, but I've only come across a few crystals that I can actually *feel*, regardless of what people say about the other ones. I love selenite. In wand or tower form, polished or unpolished, doesn't matter. When I touch selenite to my skin and ask it to take away negative energy, I can feel it happening. And because I believe it, that makes the effect even stronger. So for some reason selenite is just my thing. It won't necessarily be yours.

I also feel connected to jewelry made of lapis lazuli and fluorite, and my pendulum is fluorite on twine instead of chain, which is more common. (A pendulum is for getting answers, not for protection. See Chapter 7 for more discussion on psychic tools for divination.)

Some people burn sage, palo santo, or incense (which is called "smudging") with the intention of letting the smoke clear their aura of outside influences and purify the energy in their homes. They may take a bath with salts or certain herbs, or use the act of showering itself as a mechanism for cleansing themselves energetically as well as physically. Have you noticed how taking a shower at the end of a rough day does more than just wash off the sweat and dirt? There's more to it than the warm water relaxing you and soothing your muscles. The water is actually clearing your energetic field, too, and also bombarding you with negative ions that have multiple beneficial effects for your physical and mental health.

Some use a cross or other religious symbol that holds personal meaning for them. Others burn candles to protect their home. (Candles are a nice lower-smoke alternative to smudging, but don't forget to make your intention strong.)

As you can see, some techniques are proactively protective while others are intended for restorative effect after the fact. Regardless of strategy, psychic protection methods have long histories spanning just about every culture and religion. You probably recognize some of the approaches I mentioned but perhaps you didn't specifically associate them with psychic protection until now.

If you just feel like there's inert negative or unwanted energy hanging around your house, you can ring a bell or walk through each room clapping. It sounds crazy, I know, but you'll hear the difference between an average chime or clap and how it sounds when you're in a spot (often a corner) where stuck energy has accumulated. Continue ringing or clapping in that area and the sound waves will break the stagnant energy up, and you'll notice the sound changes.

Even just the ordinary act of opening your windows and cleaning the house can usher out unwanted energy.

Maintaining a positive, flowing space is a strong first line of defense. It's like having a healthy physical body—you're more likely to stay well during flu season than someone who's already run down.

Maybe candles, sage, and salts feel too magicky for you. Or too pagan. Whatever. It's fine not to use them. Or any tools at all really. And while I agree that stones, blessed candles, and the other paraphernalia associated with spiritual practice have intrinsic properties, I still assert confidently that the biggest factor in protection is one's intention to be protected.

For the vast majority of people, visualizations will be adequate. But if the idea of a sacred or symbolic object, candles, incense, or any of these items resonate with you or your partner, check out your options online or visit a local metaphysical bookshop. The people who work there are eagerly awaiting a chance to talk to you about psychic protection tools.

Good for you but essential for them

I am a huge proponent of psychic protection for everybody, but to be entirely honest, this type of protection is even more critical for your partner, the practicing psychic, than it is for you. They're more susceptible to negative energies in our everyday world and they might also be very sensitive to the energies of other dimensions, where they become more vulnerable than we are here.

Different people like different methods but in general, ones that make us feel empowered are best, in contrast to methods that cause us to feel a decrease in control because we're giving away our power to an outside source in exchange for protection.

By taking charge of our own psychic protection processes, we grow stronger. And when you or your partner notice a positive outcome from using psychic protection, it will be great validation that the skills of intention and visualization make a perceptible impact on your lives.

Consequently, it's important that you help your significant other find and practice methods that work for them. Remember, the only wrong way to do it is to have a lack of intention. Plus using techniques that are aggressive, offensive, or hostile toward others is not preferred and will often get you in trouble, but everything else is legitimate and fair game.

You'll probably be happy to hear that the routines associated with psychic protection skills generally become less labor intensive, requiring less conscious effort as one gets stronger. You may hear accomplished psychics talk about "set it and forget it" when discussing their protection mechanisms. This means they don't always work through a visualization or protocol, they merely check on their grounding and other protections periodically to make sure they're intact.

Don't let this give you an excuse to be lax in the beginning, though. There is value in mastering the basics, as with any art or discipline worth learning.

Chapter 7

GEARING UP (TOOLS)

Depending on what types of abilities are emerging for your loved one, there may be tools that are frequently associated with those modalities. For example, many psychics use tarot cards, but often in their own unique ways. If you visit two psychics who "read your cards," you may find that the only thing in common in the sessions is that there are cards involved. However, using tarot or any tool is always just a personal choice, not a requirement for being a "real" psychic.

Sometimes ordinary people who aren't even psychic use these items, too, like the farmers and cowboys who've used dowsing rods for centuries (if not millennia) to figure out where to dig wells.

There are many items, like crystals, that you've probably seen around town without even looking for them. Regular gift shops now sell paraphernalia that used to be considered the purview of fortune tellers and witches, so it's really easy to get your hands on anything you might want.

I still think a metaphysical store is a better place to shop until you become well-acquainted with your loved one's "kit" or "gear" (to co-opt military terminology), though, because the employees of those specialized stores are generally knowledgeable about the proper usage of the products they sell.

This is not to suggest, however, that your neighborhood grocery checker, your waiter, your auto mechanic, or the person running the daycare down the street couldn't tell you a lot about this stuff. Metaphysics is becoming mainstream. You might be shocked to find out how many people around you can speak in an informed way about items commonly used in psychic practice or protection.

I propose that you help your loved one research these tools: their pros and cons, their proper usages, and any inherent dangers of using them. (Aside from a Ouija board, I think that most of these items are safe for most people as long as you have positive intention, but it is far from my place to tell you what tools are going to feel right for you.)

Comfort levels are why I am suggesting that you take an active role, or at least a supportive role, in researching whichever of these tools are relevant for or of interest to your significant other. Or yourself, since you too can use many of these tools to enhance your own intuition and begin developing the latent ability that inevitably lies within you.

Or perhaps neither of you will be interested in any tools at all, which is also completely fine.

But the more involved you are in the process, the more comfortable you will be with the outcomes. On the other hand, if the psychic/healer is forced to handle it all on their own, some of their decisions are not going to be to your liking. Not intentionally, but simply from the lack of your input.

For example, would you mind bringing friends home to a smoky house because your significant other is ritually smudging with sage? If that would bother you, talk about it ahead of time. Don't assume they'll just know. It will make life a lot easier on both of you to head off conflict and make decisions as a team.

Tools of the trade

Here is a cursory introduction to some common tools used in psychic/healing work. The list is certainly not exhaustive but will give you a basic understanding of the range of ways people use tools to obtain information and stimulate their psychic senses.

Cards (tarot, angel, oracle, etc.) — There are two main ways that people use cards:
- They learn the standardized meaning for each card and then interpret it accordingly when it comes up in a spread. (A spread refers to the pattern in which the cards are laid out. Some people like formal configurations while others are more casual about it and just lay the cards on the table wherever feels right as they're asking questions.) Note that this approach can be used by anyone, even people who reject the idea that they are psychic, because it requires only dedication to study and no conscious use of intuition.
- They use the cards more loosely as a trigger mechanism, allowing their intuitive knowing to surface as they look over the displayed cards. This approach requires

acceptance of and attunement with one's intuitive abilities.

One of our favorite psychics uses a combination of these methods. She has multiple decks shuffled together and throws down cards in a slow, almost continuous rhythm while she's talking to our Guides to get the answers we're seeking. Occasionally she'll pick out one card from the growing mound on the table and explain its significance for us, but most she just registers silently to herself and moves on. I have no idea what her process is and she can barely articulate why she does this herself but it works for her and she's amazing at her job so she's just going with it.

Scrying tools (crystal ball, mirror)—Scrying involves eliminating distractions and then softening one's focus to gaze into or almost through the scrying surface, upon which images will ultimately appear, providing messages or information for the reader. This is a significantly oversimplified description, of course, but gives you the gist of the process.

I've never tried scrying. It seems like extra work to me. And I might actually be a little spooked if I saw an image appear in a mirror or crystal ball. But I realize that some people like ritual and paraphernalia so again, it's just a personal choice and we all have to figure out what methods work best for us regardless of what anyone else says.

Pendulum or dowsing/divining rods—As I mentioned earlier, I carry a pendulum in my purse in a pretty little bag, and though I only break it out occasionally now, I love having it with me all the time regardless.

Pendulums are simple, consisting of something heavy—usually with a point—hanging on the end of a string or chain. It doesn't have to be any particular item though crystals are the most popular while other people prefer metal pendants. They're used for everything from double-checking answers in daily matters to helping locate missing people.

Dowsing or diving rods are simple L-shaped items you hold loosely in each hand, pointed away from you, and when you find the target you're looking for they start to cross or swing apart. There's also a Y-shaped rod, where you hold two parts in your hands and the third part moves up or down when you've found your target.

Rods, like pendulums, don't need to be made from any specific material. In fact, you can pick up a Y-shaped branch or bend two pieces of wire hanger into L's and they'll work just as well as commercially designed products.

Traditionally they were used for finding water but can be used to pinpoint just about anything.

Both of these tools work mainly on a binary system. Yes/no, A/B, etc. Even when finding something on a map or body, the pendulum or rods will be in the neutral position and will react when you get to the right place, which is basically like off/on. So keep this in mind when using those tools. They're useful for the right jobs but are going to give you information in a limited way.

Crystals—Many healers use crystals on or near the bodies of their clients to either absorb or radiate certain energetic frequencies that will help remedy that person's issues. Most psychics don't use crystals to obtain their information, but will often use them as psychic or energetic protection during a session and at other times, as mentioned in the previous chapter.

Casting tools (I Ching, runes, Celtic ogham, tea leaves) — These are likely the oldest divination tools in existence, dating back millennia. Sometimes the sticks, stones, coins, tea leaves or other items are read by correlating their images or patterns to a standard text or set of well-defined results; other times they are simply used to inspire the intuition of the reader. Much like cards, actually.

Ouija board (aka talking board) — I agree with most folks in the paranormal community that Ouija boards are a bad idea. As much as I would like to leave it at that because it seems self-evident to me, I suppose I should elaborate on my opinion.

A big part of the problem is that most people treat them like a toy or game. They're hoping for some unseen force to push the planchette around the board, but they don't consider the potential danger they might pose to themselves and others.

Certainly not every experience with a Ouija board is going to bring negative consequences. There are many things that could happen, including nothing at all. There's also the possibility that one person will be intentionally tricking the other. And in some cases, the ideomotor effect will be in play: when your expectation is so strong for a certain result that your body and subconscious act of their own accord to give you the expected outcome and you are not even aware of it coming from yourself.

But sometimes a legitimate connection is made with the other side.

When using a Ouija board, everybody is a little excited, nervous, skeptical. Who knows what's going through their minds. You're combining these unstable energies with the intention to draw entities into your space. Occasionally, one actually shows up. And too often when we open that particular door, we don't have control over who comes through it.

For some reason, Ouija boards seem to attract energies that aren't generally welcome here or who have it in their personality or makeup to derive power from the fear of others. Whether they are stuck spirits (i.e. ghosts) with a bad attitude or things more ominous, just leave them all outside and don't invite them into your house.

Data-based systems (astrology, numerology, palmistry) — These modalities, like learning the standardized meaning of a tarot card or an I Ching hexagram, can be used even by those who don't consider themselves psychic. Basic elements of these systems, especially astrology, are already prevalent in our pop culture. When was the last time you met someone who didn't know their own astrological sign? Have you ever? I don't think I have.

To really master these systems takes years of diligent study, but you can learn the foundational elements — enough to impress or annoy people at parties — by reading a book or two or searching for tutorials online.

I personally think that despite the fact that these techniques rely largely on a specific knowledge base, they too are means for sparking the practitioner's intuition, and that once proficient with the system the reader often can provide more information than is just listed in a book of charts.

So you can see, tools can be fun. Many of them are quite beautiful to look at. And some people feel more powerful and effective when using them. But remember, they're entirely optional.

Chapter 8

TAKING CARE OF YOURSELF

When Brett read my first draft of this book he said, "Wow, you make it seem like a lot of work."

"It has been," I replied. I don't think that was the answer he was expecting but it's the truth.

I didn't want to dishonor myself by denying that supporting him through his spiritual awakening and psychic development had been taxing (especially in the beginning). Not necessarily more so than supporting someone through other major life changes, but certainly on par.

But that's not to say that it's work all the time. Every topic I've touched on in the book has affected us to a greater or lesser extent, so that's why I know to include them all for your benefit. But honestly, not every day brings an assault on my belief system, a concern for Brett's stability, or an uncomfortable conversation with a hostile skeptic. In fact these things happen less and less frequently as time passes—as we embrace this life as just "what is" and as the once extraordinary becomes the familiar.

The duration of the difficult part of the journey with your significant other may be shorter or longer than ours was, depending on the specifics of your situation and how you each comport yourselves. There are things you should do, however, to support, inform, and uplift yourself in the meantime. They'll enhance your life overall and make the occasional burdens feel lighter.

Don't worry that they can read your mind

First of all, do not waste any time worrying that you are going to lose the privacy of your inner world just because your partner demonstrates some psychic talent now. While it's true that various types of sensitives can pick up on your emotions, it's unlikely that anyone can actually read your mind. Even if their ability is telepathy, that doesn't mean they can read minds all the time or on command or against the subject's will. It doesn't really work that way.

And even when someone has some telepathic skills, it's often significantly more difficult to do a reading of someone they're close to because they know too much about that person so their conscious mind gets in the way.

In the next chapter, which is about psychic modalities, I talk about telepathic-type moments as normal byproducts of being close to someone. These instances of "thought sharing" still don't demonstrate that the person can forcibly read your mind, though. It's more like having the same thought at the same time. This phenomenon is fun and also gives us personal experiences to confirm the validity of psychic ability, but they don't prove that anyone can enter your mind intentionally and invasively without your agreement.

And while empaths and telepaths may be adept at sensing when you're lying or hiding something, any person good at interpreting body language or "reading people" would be able to figure it out anyway without any identified psychic ability, so this is basically a moot point.

The bottom line is that you don't need to worry about your personal security systems being compromised. You still have the same privacy and sovereignty over your inner kingdom that you had before.

Kick back and watch TV

If you have a TV, you've probably noticed that there are so many psychic and paranormal shows now that you could live permanently on your couch and never have to watch the same thing twice. You may enjoy some, all, or none of them, depending on your tastes in programming.

But I want you to actively seek out some movies and TV shows that highlight a person or family who has adjusted to living with psychic ability. Non-fiction, documentary, or reality shows when possible. Not just programs about ghost hunting or Bigfoot. Ideally, shows or movies that feature a psychic's family life or incorporate more about the psychic on a personal level instead of just showing them doing readings. As always, take in what resonates with you and disregard the rest.

There are lots of these shows and most have the same take-away message: that by having the right attitude and embracing this change, instead of fighting or rejecting it, you can actually have a very happy life; likely one that is even richer than before.

I hope you can find some time in the near future to tune into at least one of them, either alone or with the family. Watching together may actually provide some great opportunities for discussion.

Maintain the infrastructure

You might have to take more control of your family's infrastructure. Or you're possibly the one handling this already. Either way, by infrastructure I mean making sure the bills are paid, the kids get to their appointments on time, there are groceries in the house, and the litter box is cleaned. You know, the stuff that allows your particular household to function.

Running a tight ship will significantly decrease your own level of stress when your partner goes through phases of being unpredictable or less reliable than usual. Having all of your other ducks in a row minimizes the impact of periodic fluctuations, allowing you to maintain a greater sense of dominion over your life due to having only one or a few crises to handle at a time.

Essentially, by keeping your routine as normal as possible, your loved one's moments of non-normalness can be handled like all of the other speed bumps that show up in your life.

Remember that this expansion is happening to people all over the world, in all strata of society. If you can't tell, that means they've incorporated the psychic realm into their lives effectively. The same is possible for you. If not in the beginning, at least after a period of adjustment you will be able to resume your familiar routines and continue building your life, just like before. You'll reach a point where you'll marvel at how far you've come and how normal it all feels.

You have survived, adapted, and overcome many challenges in the past and this is no different. But it will be much easier to stay on track if the foundation hasn't fallen apart in the meantime, so keep that infrastructure intact.

Be flexible

Here's something you've probably heard before (it's called the Serenity Prayer):

Grant me the serenity to accept the things I cannot change,
the courage to change the things I can,
and the wisdom to know the difference.

It's clear your world may be changing, and I propose that it's changing for the better in the long run (even if it's uncomfortable right now). Keeping as flexible a mindset as possible will make the awkward part of the transition shorter and less difficult, allowing you to move on to the part where life feels relatively under control again. To whatever degree life is ever really under control.

Ever since the metaphysical started occupying center stage in our life, I've often found myself saying, "Hmm. Well, I guess that's OK" about things I would not have thought were OK when I was younger. So either I have mellowed with age, learned to hone in on only what's really important, or had my defenses broken down by frequently experiencing things I previously thought were impossible. It's probably some combination thereof.

Through this growth experience, what I have realized is that flexibility, or relinquishing the need for absolute control, is the real strength. Rigidity leaves you with only two options: either you successfully stand your ground or you lose and break. On the other hand, flexibility allows for making the best of any situation and is an essential element of that life-saving characteristic known as resilience.

Regardless of where the ability and strength to maintain this mindset come from, relaxing your need for control is beneficial in almost every scenario. For example, kids seldom turn out to be exactly who parents expected or even hoped for. Yet when a parent is open minded and accepting and can let go of "supposed to be," they almost always realize their kids are even more amazing than they could have dreamed up. But when a parent is stuck on the idea that the child is not living up to their preconceived expectations, that same amazing child is viewed as a disappointment and their fragile life is ruined accordingly.

Applying this same philosophy to your current situation will go a long way in making it seem like an adventure instead of a catastrophe. Choosing to let uncomfortable and unfamiliar circumstances be OK takes away their power to upset you and gives you the freedom to be responsive instead of reactive.

So paradoxically, giving up the need for control is actually what gives you back some control.

Let it go

I've learned from various sources, including psych school, hypnotherapists, Deepak Chopra books, etc., that thoughts and feelings are actually energy. Fortunately, that means when just deciding to not let something bother us doesn't do the trick, there are techniques you can use to release upset energy out of the mind and body so its effects don't linger. I can't emphasize enough how helpful this knowledge has been in processing my own worries and emotions.

Letting go of thoughts or feelings is similar to clearing one's mind during meditation except you can do it anytime, anywhere, with just a simple visualization. It doesn't take a quiet space or a timer or a blocked-out appointment on your calendar, so it's actually even easier than meditating.

Your intention to let go is of primary importance. Turn inward and explain to yourself that you intend to let go of whatever this idea or feeling is that's bothering you. Then you can just visualize steam (that represents what you want to get rid of) evaporating out of your body. Or maybe you prefer the imagery of sawdust being vacuumed out of your body. Or you can turn your unwanted thoughts and feelings into butterflies, who flit away gently.

Whichever approach you take, don't force anything out—that creates resistance and tension. Just allow the thoughts and feelings to leave by not holding on to them. Let the process take however long it takes, and then notice how you feel better after it's all cleared out.

It might take practice if this is a new idea but eventually you will be able to viscerally sense the absence of the unwanted energy in your body and psyche after you've released it consciously.

Some people use meditation, yoga, running, working out, knitting, fishing, cooking, cleaning, art, playing with their dog, holding their grandchild, or dancing to alleviate their stress. It doesn't matter what you do to relieve stress, just make sure you're doing it. You deserve to be healthy and happy and stress is the opposite of that.

Remember that YOU are the protagonist of your story

Your life is not on hold just because your partner is having challenges. From the moment you're born until the moment you die, you are the only constant in your own life, so be sure to take care of yourself first and foremost.

Even when we sometimes sacrifice for others, we are not and should never be the sidekicks or supporting characters in our own stories. It's easy to forget sometimes but nobody truly benefits by us losing ourselves to serve them—not us, not our partners, not even our children—and despite how most of this book might sound, I am not suggesting you do so.

You have to find ways to balance your loved one's growth with the countless elements that comprise your own life instead of letting their needs occupy too much of your energy and mindspace. This is why in earlier chapters I've mentioned still going to the movies, concerts, or county fair if you want to go, even if they don't want to.

This will be easy or hard, depending on personality type. Some of us are raised to be nurturers and to derive our worth from what we do for others, while some have mainly been encouraged to strive for achievement. Both approaches have significant value for the individual and we need both types of people in the world. And every type in between.

Those of you who are already comfortable with the idea of taking care of yourself first—you've got this covered. But for those of you who tend to subordinate your own needs to the wants of others, I hope we can move you past that.

Aside from the reality that taking care of ourselves is actually good for the people around us (but we're trying to focus on you now), the mere fact that you exist means you're entitled—and even expected—to take care of yourself. On all levels (physical, mental, emotional, spiritual). Regardless of any illegitimate claims others may have made to the contrary.

I mean really, when was the last time you heard someone called "martyr" in a good way?

If this concept of prioritizing yourself is causing you emotional or psychological discomfort, I encourage you to really look at that. It's an issue you need to resolve not only for yourself but also your family and certainly your children, if you have any. They learn more from example than from what they're told, so if you insist on not prioritizing your own needs, that's the lesson they're picking up.

If someone in your life is still trying to convince you that their needs and wants are more important than your own, that you somehow "owe" them that kind of sacrifice, you need to find a way to either correct that situation or get away from that person.

Keep doing the things you enjoy

The first unexpected next-level wave of Brett's abilities hit while we were on summer break from our school jobs. This was fortunate timing because it allowed me to be there for him (and essentially, monitor him) 24/7 for those few weeks. And thank goodness because it was necessary. Everything really does work out when viewed in retrospect.

But except for that critical initial period, I have made sure to work on my own projects and see my own friends and try new things when I want to. I do volunteer work. I go to conferences. I go to movies and events by myself or with someone else if he doesn't want to go. I even make it clear when I just need some space.

And Brett is all in favor of this because he loves me enough to want the best for me, but also because he fell in love with a person with certain interests, traits, and drives, and he doesn't want me to give up those independent parts of myself. Obviously we share many activities and passions but not absolutely everything. This keeps us interesting to each other and not resentful about losing ourselves.

All couples should be aware of maintaining that balance. Make sure you're always doing what you want to do, just for you, so it doesn't feel like you've turned into mere extensions of each other and you don't become unrecognizable from the people you were before (which is what brought you together in the first place).

Capitalize on opportunities for growth

One way I have capitalized on the changes brought to our life by Brett's development was deciding to pursue whatever abilities of my own were emerging, rather than just considering myself an accessory to his experience. I love learning, I love growing, I love being presented with out-of-the-box ideas for consideration. So this has been a perfect opportunity for me to venture into an area I probably wouldn't have on my own.

It's kind of like someone exposing you to new music or an ethnic food you've never tried. Maybe you won't like it, and that's OK. But maybe you'll love it. So go ahead and acknowledge any changes that are bubbling up within yourself now. Just try them on and then notice how it feels. Is it kind of exciting? Or is the idea of growing and changing too scary?

Change is hard for a lot of people and I'll admit to having only an average tolerance for it myself. It's easy for me to expand my thought process when I get new information and to make reasonable shifts in how I operate, but if change means suddenly living without someone or something I'm attached to, or switching jobs or living arrangements not of my own volition, then suddenly I'm not so excited about the concept of change anymore.

But sometimes we have to tolerate that our boundaries will be pushed a little, and at other times we have to consciously expand our own comfort zones. If we honestly reflect on our lives, we can see that most positively life-changing experiences have involved stepping out of our comfort zone to some degree. Many events or opportunities that seemed random or unwelcome at the time in retrospect seem like perfectly aligned stepping stones along the path to where we are now. Thank goodness we walked through those doors when they opened before us.

Recognizing a spark of psychic or healing ability within yourself is not just potentially exciting, it can even be empowering. These personal glimpses into the interconnectedness of the Universe, of something larger than ourselves, of being a person actively participating in human evolution, these are powerful on all levels of your existence.

Throughout history, some people have been changed forever by a single metaphysical occurrence. Think about the old stories people told of seeing a ghost once or hearing a little disembodied voice that helped them avert disastrous consequences. One experience often changed their worldview. When towns were smaller, this type of story was enough to establish local legends.

We've come a long way, collectively. I realize that on a personal level, one-off experiences are still quite meaningful and special to the beholder. But these days many people are having frequent or continuous experiences and are fully incorporating them into their regular lives with minimal observable effect because it's becoming normalized.

And I understand that just because something is becoming more commonplace doesn't mean it isn't still scary, potentially. Buying a house, getting married, having a child—what could be more common than that? But yet those are still nerve racking for most people because they involve commitment to being significantly different in the future, and with no guarantees of success. Your exploration of psychic abilities is fairly minor in comparison, right? So don't worry too much, just jump in.

Let yourself be lifted up

Since I had been playing around with animal communication for a few years before Brett really started using his psychic abilities in a major way, it was probably easier for me to decide to tinker around with other modalities than it might be for someone who is new to the whole psychic thing to decide to take the first step. But don't forget that I, too, was once new to the whole psychic thing.

I'm not one of these professed "natural-born psychics" who say they've always been able to do whatever. I opened up to the possibility and reality through a conscious decision and concerted effort, which is why I know you can too and how I know it's worth it.

Now that I've decided to accept that psychic ability is the birthright of all humans, the skills that Brett and other psychics are practicing rub off on me when I'm around them. Essentially I'm allowing my vibration to be raised by those who are already operating at a higher frequency. It's like the resonance of tuning forks.

We can feel a similar mechanism in our everyday lives. Do you feel physically better associating with happy, positive people? On the other hand, do you have those friends or family who "drag you down" when they're around? They're perpetually bummed out and you can actually feel heaviness and negativity in your body when you've spent time with them. It's not your imagination. Your energy is entraining to theirs, for better or worse. We can use psychic protection to help guard against being dragged down but when we're not in active self-defense mode, entrainment just happens naturally and impacts how we feel.

Remember what I said about empaths and crowds? Those who are empathic often physically cannot stand the bombardment of energy that comes from being around so many people at once because it's like someone turned up the atmospheric pressure on them. Or they experience the range of others' emotions as if they were having their own severe mood swing.

Have I mentioned lately that I don't think being an empath sounds like very much fun?

Anyway, take that same concept of resonance or entrainment and think of applying it in a positive way. It's like a drug-free, second-hand high that happens when you open yourself to receiving graceful bumps up in your own frequency by being around people who are already "elevated." Similar to becoming excited when you're around someone who is excited about something, even though you might not care as much as they do.

So just by being around more spiritually advanced people, you will find that you probably feel better and may even start to experience the beginning phases of psychic ability yourself.

You can also learn a lot, in an academic sense, from any of these people who are at least one step ahead of wherever you are now. They don't have to be masters of a craft or experts in a particular subject. It's often the people who are just a little farther along the path that we learn the most from.

I find this with teachers a lot, and not just in the metaphysical realm. Though I may be awed by people who can speak authoritatively about impressive subjects, if what they're talking about is too far over my head I don't learn much because there's a big gap in my understanding.

But when someone is just a few steps ahead of me in a particular skill (or is talking to me at that level instead of at the peak of their own knowledge), that's when I can really grasp and absorb what they have to share.

To use an analogy, when someone takes karate lessons, they don't start with the black-belt moves. They might appreciate watching a master's demonstration but they need to build their own skills incrementally. This applies to just about every endeavor. Unless you're some kind of savant, you don't start with calculus, you start with algebra and work your way up. The same is true for psychic ability.

But even if you're not looking to build your own skills, let the "good vibes" put out by psychics rub off and improve your day whenever you get a chance.

Trust that it's worth the risk

Despite all of my persuading, maybe you still think you don't want to develop any of your own abilities. Maybe you feel that one person in the house acting "crazy" is already enough of a disruption to your life. Or maybe you're watching your loved one struggle at this early stage and figure you want no part of it.

Even if this is how you feel right now, I highly encourage you to reconsider for a couple of reasons (besides the fact that it's pretty darn cool once you get the hang of it).

One is that anything you can do to corroborate what your partner is saying will make it easier for you to accept their claims. If you're harboring doubts right now, being able to validate what they're telling you will be a huge relief for both of you.

Another is that in addition to the potential fun and stimulation of developing your own abilities, doing so can kick your bonding with your partner up to a whole 'nother level.

The relationship dynamic I'm referring to is basically "bonding through adversity," which sometimes happens when people live through an adventure or trauma together. The intensity of the situation causes them to develop an emotional bond that exceeds what exists between them and others who weren't part of it. They survived a significant, life-changing event and feel that only someone else who has shared that experience can really understand them anymore.

It's like the common movie plot about a family or a married couple in a rut, who are presented with a series of challenges that push them way out of their comfort zones to survive a potentially disastrous outcome. In the process they grow individually but also together, and their relationships are reinvigorated for having had that mutual experience.

Everything is relative so even though your current scenario is probably not as extreme as most movie plots, this is still a legitimate relationship-building opportunity. Being an active participant in your partner's life-changing journey can have that same bonding effect because you will be developing together while also growing as individuals.

If you're not convinced about the importance of this, consider how often "we just grew apart" is given as the reason for couples splitting up. Of course I'm not saying that your relationship will crumble if you don't follow my advice, I'm just pointing out that this is one of the kinds of situations that can divide people if they don't at least find common ground.

Your significant other may progress more rapidly than you (or vice versa) and that's OK. Don't succumb to jealousy or destructive competitiveness. Evolution is a process of expanding your self-definition. Just like nobody's body is going to take to a workout regimen quite the same way, neither will your psychic muscles develop exactly like anyone else's.

It's easy to ignore or rationalize away a lot of these phenomena at first so don't succumb to that. Notice. Participate. Wonder. Embrace the idea that there are still things worth learning. Be more open to your intuition.

Let your loved one teach you their process and play around with it together to see if you get results, too. Or study an entirely different skill that seems like a better fit for you, regardless of what they're doing.

Get your own support

Maybe you've learned to handle the situation by this point so now it's just something you gripe about when you meet up with your friends for lunch or cocktails. That's great. That's what we're aiming for, as long as it's giving you what you need and you're not wearing anybody's patience thin.

However, if you're still experiencing stress, trepidation, resentment, overwhelm, or any other emotion that is disrupting your mental, emotional, or physical well-being, you need to get more serious about taking care of yourself.

Depending on where you live perhaps you can find some new friends who are going through the same shift. Previously I mentioned using Meetup.com and other websites for helping your partner find camaraderie. You can use the same types of resources for yourself. And if you stop by a metaphysical bookstore they might have suggestions for when and where to meet some new people that will understand your situation.

But if you think you need more help than friends can provide, this might be a good time to consider therapy. Or at least a structured support group.

In case you're worried about the outdated idea that there might be a stigma associated with seeing a therapist, I assure you that the perception of therapy has changed significantly over the last decade or two. In fact, in some areas it's considered a positive thing; an indication that people are willing to work on improving themselves.

But if you'd still feel uncomfortable sharing the fact that you're in therapy with anyone outside of your nuclear family, guess what? You don't have to tell anybody! You can see a therapist just the same as you can see a medical specialist or a closet organizer or a hair stylist and it's not anybody's business. So don't worry about that.

Now in case you've never sought out a therapist before, let me share a few tips that I've learned from sitting on both sides of that room.

Know thyself. Understand the different approaches and seek out a practitioner who works in whatever way you prefer. Do you want someone who focuses strictly on changing behavior or do you want someone who is going to listen to your thoughts and feelings for a whole session? Do you want a counselor who incorporates dream analysis, art, hypnosis, or even dance into their work? Someone who talks and interacts a lot or someone who sits silently and lets you talk the whole time? There are a lot more modalities than most people realize and not all of them are going to suit you, so become an informed consumer. This is 100% about what you need or want.

Not all therapists are created equal. Make sure your therapist is going to be comfortable talking about what you want to talk about. As professionals, therapists are supposed to be able to field whatever you throw at them and for the most part, they can. But that doesn't mean it's their strength or that they enjoy working on your particular issue, in which case you may not get the biggest bang for your buck or you might not be a client they look forward to seeing (which you will definitely end up feeling at some point and it doesn't feel good).

For example, there are counselors who specialize in sexual issues while others just approach sexual dysfunction by doing general talk therapy because they aren't trained or equipped to facilitate an ongoing, in-depth course of treatment focused specifically on that subject. They may not even personally be comfortable with sexuality so they'd be constantly tempering their internal reactions for the client's sake. Substance abuse is another obvious example. It's almost unheard of for a substance counselor to not be a recovering addict themselves because it's fundamental that a therapist can connect with the client's experience. You don't want someone who sees issues in generic terms.

So try to determine whether the therapists you're considering are not just skilled in run-of-the-mill relationship-based issues but are also genuinely open-minded about what you believe is going on in your house. If they cannot accept even the possibility of what you are saying as true then you're setting up a situation where your therapist is giving the appearance of supporting you outwardly but always harbors doubts about your sanity, intelligence, or veracity.

One way to determine this is to listen to your gut instinct about whether they are privately judging you. You won't want to stick with a person who makes you feel bad about yourself, even subconsciously. But make sure you're not "projecting" your own judgment onto them and assuming that they feel a certain way about what you're saying just because you feel that way on some level. It takes some self-awareness to identify when we're projecting but it's a skill worth cultivating.

Try out more than one therapist. Take them for a test drive by having an initial consultation or first session with more than one. Preferably three but at least two. It's easy to feel obligated to stay with the first person you try out because they're just so darn nice to you. Just be honest and upfront with them about your plan to shop around. They're used to this.

Believe it or not, they think it's healthy. It means that on some level you know how to honor your own needs instead of being a doormat. It means you're less likely to be playing the victim card because you can be proactive on your own behalf and that's going to make their work easier and more productive.

If a therapist can't handle the idea of competition then they haven't learned to handle their own insecurities so what good are they going to do for you anyway?

Get to the point (Part 1). Tell the prospective therapists why you're there in that first session or consultation and see how they work with it. That's going to give you a better sense of who you should sign on with than skirting around the real issue for a while then realizing later that they can't really handle your situation.

Don't worry, therapists have confidentiality privileges with their clients so whatever you say to them behind closed doors (aside from "physical danger to self or others") has to stay with them.

Get to the point (Part 2). Once you're working with someone, dive in. Don't waste your time and money being modest or bashful or deliberating about when the right time is to share what's on your mind. Get to the point, starting with the first session, and starting at the beginning of each session after that.

And here's a therapy optimization trick that most people won't tell you, maybe because they haven't figured it out: Skip the story and go straight to the feelings. So many clients waste most of their sessions complaining and being stuck on the "he said, she said, I said," and they don't get anywhere because all they did was rehash a story they've already told their friends anyway and then their time is up.

When your butt hits the couch in the therapy room, you should be leading with something like, "I'm frustrated and annoyed because no matter how many times I ask him to do X, he always forgets or blows it off" or "I found out she tells her friends everything about us and now I don't feel like I can trust her." Your therapist will be trying to move you to this point so work can begin anyway, so do it yourself and you won't have wasted 30 of your 50 minutes.

Keep your eyes on the prize

Relationship strife of varying degrees is common at this point, especially if your paradigm doesn't expand along with theirs. You might find that unfair, and I hear where you're coming from. Your life together was built on agreement about or at least compromise between your belief systems. It's usually one of the most foundational elements of a relationship and of each person's identity. And now you might feel like they're not holding up their end of the bargain.

Whether or not to follow your partner down that path is no small consideration. I appreciate that. My lack of religious upbringing probably made it easier for me to entertain and even embrace a broader range of phenomena and entities (we irreverently call them "the cast of characters") once I opened my mind to it, but remember that I had to come all the way from the starting point of atheism.

It's how I was known in my community. I spent years making vehement arguments in defense of it. In the Navy I got a never-ending barrage of harassment over it. And at the time I was doing that, it felt like I was standing for what was right. Until I opened my mind to new knowledge and experience and realized that the Universe is so much more complicated and diverse and full than any of us are taught.

No religion or philosophy has it all figured out. Not even science. And even their parts that are correct still only show us a little piece of the really big picture.

Accepting this more inclusive (and more probable) view of reality gave me the strength to change my public persona with gradually increasing confidence. Sure, I get grief from some friends who used to know me as a dogmatic adherent to "observable and replicable." Especially those who are still stuck there. But others are curious or even have their own stories to share because they're on a path of growth now, too.

And though certain friendships have faded away due to irreconcilable differences in our worldviews, I have made just as many new friends who "get it" and those are the kinds of people I'd rather be around now anyway.

In the difficult moments, bring your thoughts back to what is most important to you, and let that be your guide. Even if where the journey leads is going to require you to stretch yourself. You can handle this. Keep your eyes on the prize and it will all turn out OK.

Leap and the net will appear

And finally, after everything I've said so far, the truth is that the biggest factor in enjoying this ride is just deciding to enjoy it.

It really comes down to that. How awesome is it that the power is entirely in your hands?

The fact that a person you're close to has emerging abilities demonstrates that there's much more to life than some people think there is. But even those of us who consider ourselves fairly spiritual can be taken aback a little by witnessing the facility with which someone we know can interact with the other planes and dimensions. And you might also be feeling a potentially unwelcome shift within yourself. It can all seem like a lot to accept and handle.

But your Higher Self wants to be on this path or it wouldn't be happening. So put your chin up and shoulders back and take the first step. And then the next. One step at a time. Fortunately, you're ready.

Chapter 9

TYPES OF PSYCHIC ABILITY

Here's an introduction to different types of psychic abilities so you can determine which of them relate to your partner's new skill set. And maybe even your own. There might be more than one for each of you and as you'll see, that's more the rule than the exception.

Basically, whether you go see a tarot card reader or a medium, they will be receiving their impressions through a range of sensory inputs that are fairly universal. And while their outward presentations to you as a client may seem very different, their internal processes may be quite similar in terms of hearing, seeing, and feeling information. On the other hand, two practitioners who seem to use the same method might be having vastly different internal experiences.

Think of each practitioner as an individualized expression of the spectrum of possibilities, sort of like how musical performances can seem significantly different from each other even though they're all based on the same foundational elements of chords, harmony, timing, etc.

This chapter will provide a solid foundational description of each psychic modality, but I can only really scratch the surface.

Each item I mention in a paragraph or two has many books written exclusively about that concept alone, so use my short guide to identify what's of interest to you and you'll easily find ample resources to expand your knowledge when you're ready.

I suggest reading all of these entries even if you feel the specific modality doesn't currently relate to you or your partner. You will benefit from having a general familiarity with all of these terms because the esoteric is rapidly becoming mainstream and you'll have many more opportunities to talk about this topic in the future than you can imagine. And besides, this is part of your life now so you may as well be able to carry on an informed conversation about it.

How to

You're most likely already receiving psychic messages from different sources and in different ways. You just aren't in the habit of paying attention to notice them for what they are.

That's why I'm going to give a brief explanation of how to start working in the various modalities throughout the chapter. However, the first step for most of them is a standard process I call "psychic readiness"—the state where you're ready to receive information in your own unique way. Unless otherwise noted, you can assume that the procedure below is the implied first step in the instructions for each section.

Psychic readiness

Some psychic hits come spontaneously, even if you don't want them to. And people who have been using their psychic abilities for a long time can often skip the formal prep and jump right in. But a beginner needs to learn to follow a procedure until the basics are internalized if they want to use psychic ability intentionally.

This is similar to many skills that we learn throughout our lives. The most successful people aren't unaware of the rules of the game, they actually know the rules well enough to figure out how to break them effectively. This applies in the psychic realm, too.

Here are the simple but important steps for establishing "psychic readiness."

1. Make sure you're in a space where you won't be interrupted or distracted.
2. Make sure you have whatever materials you may need, such as a notebook or your pendulum.
3. When you're settled, close your eyes and take a few deep breaths to help you focus on your body in the present moment. Breathe comfortably until you're mostly free of thoughts popping up.
4. Ground yourself, either with the roots visualization (mentioned in Chapter 6) or any other technique that works for you.
5. Set the intention to be protected during this exercise. Surround yourself with white light or use other symbolism that represents peace and safety to you. (Also discussed in Chapter 6.)
6. Set the intention to be successful during this exercise.
7. Continue breathing and allowing distracting thoughts to evaporate, until your mind is quiet and clear and you feel yourself to be in a fairly blank state of mind.

At this point you have basically achieved your "psychic readiness" state.

From here forward, until you decide to disengage, you need to trust the answers, information, or sensations you get. You're going to feel like you're just making it up. It often won't make sense. It doesn't matter at this stage. This happens to all of us, especially at first. Just go with it. But this is the line in the sand: Either you start accepting that you're getting psychic information or you reject it. If you want to come to the party, all you have to do is accept the invitation.

Types of psychic ability (*listed alphabetically*)

Animal communication: Often called *pet psychic*. (Different than an *animal whisperer,* who employs in-person training techniques and body language to solve perceived problems through behavior modification.)

This is my main personal toehold in the psychic realm. It is tremendously rewarding to give animals a voice and often times, make a lasting impact on the way people view and value them.

Animal communicators actually speak telepathically with animals. In this way, animal communication contrasts with some of the other psychic modalities where the practitioner is receiving information *about* a subject instead of having a conversation *with* someone. ("Someone" being an animal in this case.)

However, we animal communicators get our input through the same modes that other types of psychics use, too. For example, I tend to hear words in English (**clairaudience**), see images transmitted by the animal (**clairvoyance**), and feel their emotions or pains (**clairsentience/empathy**).

Does this make me clairvoyant or clairaudient then? I suppose the argument could be made, but I just consider myself an animal communicator. This is only the first example of many (since it's the very first entry on my list) of what I mentioned before: that all of these seemingly distinct abilities and experiences are not really distinct after all.

I prefer to work from a photograph, not in person. It's how I was trained and also fits with my lifestyle. But some communicators are the opposite: they really want to be there in person or on the phone so they can ask a lot of questions along the way. Personally, I like to work "cold" or "blind," with no backstory about the animal or owner. That way my clients can always be sure the information I'm giving them isn't just a deduction or rehashing of what they already told me. These different working styles are reflections of our personalities as much as functions of our abilities. None is better than the other, it's all just about optimizing our skill sets to do some really cool stuff.

How to: To use my photograph method, after making sure I'm in psychic readiness mode (which takes a lot less effort after so much practice), I look into the animal's eyes and start talking to them in my head. I introduce myself. I often pay them a compliment about their appearance or some detail the pet parent has shared. I explain that I'm talking to them to get answers for their person and am not going to be judgmental or personally involved. I keep talking until I finally "hear" an answer back to one of my questions, and that's how I know the connection is established.

The answer might come in the form of a single word. "Yes," "OK," "Hi." It might be that I start feeling physical or emotional sensations that I know aren't my own. I might get unexpected images in my head that relate to what I've been talking about.

This is the point at which I can either say, "I'm just making it up," which would shut down the connection, or I can trust that something amazing is really happening and build upon it with more questions and more conversation. This is what makes me an animal communicator and someone else, with equal potential but no trust in the process, not an animal communicator.

I always write everything down verbatim—words, feelings, images—and provide that complete transcript to my client. Not everyone does. It makes me slower than some others—those who work over the phone, for example, generally tell the pet parent what they're getting in the moment, without recording it.

Even the stuff that doesn't make sense to me is important to document because there might be a single word or phrase that turns on a lightbulb for the client. Or when an animal uses language that I wouldn't use, that's great validation for me that I really am tuned in to another consciousness. Like when a dog told me, "I can't just power down at night, I'm not a machine," I knew I had to write that down word for word because I (correctly) figured that "power down" must be a phrase the person used with them when trying to get them to settle down, which was part of the issue they were working on.

Being meticulous helps me feel comfortable that I'm not forgetting to tell the client anything and it's also good because that way they can review the transcript as many times as they want.

Many clients report crying while reading the verbatim conversations because they can feel their animal's personality coming through the words. They're often blown away by the details I provide that I couldn't possibly know if I wasn't talking directly to their pets. These things might get lost if I just interpreted and summarized the dialogue.

But when I talk to my own animals, it's a lot less formal, of course.

I like talking to non-domesticated animals like seagulls and squirrels, too. They're bursting with personality and attitude. You might think we're at the top of the hierarchy but they wouldn't necessarily agree with you, and they're not afraid to make their opinion on the subject clear.

You can talk to animals, too. Ask one a question in your mind and just trust whatever answer you get. That's how you start.

Astral projection/Out-of-Body Experiences (OBEs): In essence, these terms refer to someone's soul (or other energetic aspects, but we'll just say the soul for now) leaving the body either through the person's intention or of its own accord.

One example of this is when people wake up from surgery or a near-death experience and can describe what happened in the room while they were supposedly completely unconscious, including knowing details they could have only seen if they were hovering on the ceiling. This has become such a common occurrence that a large percentage of hospital staff have accepted the phenomenon as legitimate, even if they have no explanation.

Many people report astral travel during sleep. To the rest of us it may just seem like they were dreaming but the difference is that they often come back with information about a place or event that they couldn't possibly know if they hadn't been there "in person."

Literature about astral projection and OBEs usually mentions a silver cord that keeps the body and traveling soul connected, regardless of distance. This is believed to be a safety mechanism that ensures the soul can easily return.

Astral projection sometimes happens spontaneously and the traveler doesn't realize it's happening until they pop back into their bodies with a jerk and regain some wakeful awareness. And a small minority of people, like Brett, can sometimes just will themselves to be somewhere else and they are. But there are techniques the rest of us can learn to reach that state on purpose.

The basic instructions for astral projection make it seem like a quick and easy process but in reality, getting to this point often takes people months of diligent practice. Don't be discouraged if your progress seems slow. That's normal.

How to: You will usually do it lying down and in a dark, quiet space because astral projection requires a deeper focus than just psychic readiness. The brain state it's associated with is called the hypnogogic state—the line right between sleep and consciousness. If it helps to achieve this level of calm and focus, you can use progressive relaxation techniques (e.g. tensing and releasing your muscles in a sequence, starting with your feet) or any visualization that brings you right to the edge of sleep but not yet fully losing conscious awareness.

Be sure to surround yourself with white light or use another method of psychic protection. You will be leaving your body so you want both the physical and energetic parts of yourself to be safe.

Once in the proper brain state, imagine yourself moving parts of your body. Don't actually physically move them, just envision flexing your muscles, raising your arm, etc., until you feel like you can mentally extract your soul body from your physical body through the will of your thought.

If this has actually happened, you may feel some strange sensations and you should also be able to look around the room you're in with a conscious, dream-like awareness, different from the perspective you have while lying down.

When you feel comfortable enough with being separate from your physical body, you can go to other parts of your house and then eventually to familiar places.

Try to observe objects from different angles than you usually see them. Later you can verify the details to find out if you were indeed seeing through your soul's eyes during an astral projection session.

To return to your body, you don't need to make the trip back in the literal way you would in the physical world. Just by thinking that you want to return, you should arrive there instantly, often with a little jolt. When you wake yourself up, do so slowly. Wiggle your toes and fingers. Open your eyes gradually when you feel completely reintegrated into your body.

Hopefully you will have picked up some confirmable information.

This is a vastly oversimplified example of a technique that works for some people. If you're truly interested in mastering astral projection, you should seek out one of the well-reviewed programs that teach it in depth or perhaps even a teacher.

Auras, seeing: This is probably one of the psychic abilities that is most familiar to, and therefore least startling to, the general population.

The concept of an aura is that we all have graduated energy fields surrounding our bodies. Science lends support to this concept by acknowledging that humans do indeed produce various types of electrical and electromagnetic energy that can be measured consistently and predictably with instrumentation, both inside of and near our bodies.

And though auras are both more complex and stronger than the energy emissions recognized by mainstream science, at least it's a good starting point for conversation between science and metaphysics.

Though I only see them as clear or milky-colored energy, for many people, auras show up in a variety of colors that are constantly in flux. Proficient aura readers learn to identify how colors and sizes of auras correspond to different moods, states of health, and personality traits.

Despite the proliferation of books explaining in great detail what each color means from the author's perspective, what I hear from people who can read auras is that what color they see and what it means to them is often unique to that individual.

Consequently, if your loved one's new ability falls under the category of seeing auras, the best way to support them is to help them develop their own catalog of color meanings instead of trying to get them to conform to any particular so-called expert's dictate.

How to: Though you'll want to make sure your mind is clear and you're fairly distraction free, you don't necessarily need to go into full psychic readiness to see auras.

To start, it helps if your subject is standing near but not against a solid dark- or light-colored wall. If possible, stand far enough away that you can easily see at least their upper body.

Once your mind is quiet, look at them with a soft or unfocused gaze. Don't strain at all, just look in the subject's direction and don't focus on any point directly. Do you remember those tessellated Magic Eye images that were popular in the '90s? If you looked at them just right you could see the 3-D images embedded in them? For some people, the proper gaze is sort of like that.

After a while, you may notice a shimmery outline around the person. Some people describe it as like the distortion that comes from heat escaping off a hot road.

Don't be frustrated if there's no color at first. That usually comes with practice. But if you can see the energy field around their body, congratulations, you just saw someone's aura!

If you don't want to experiment with someone else until you're feeling more confident, you can do the same exercise with your own hand held as far away from your face as possible with a solid light or dark background.

Channeling (trance): "Channeling" is a term that is used loosely (and incorrectly) to refer to lots of different types of psychic activities. However, the true and specific meaning of channeling is to have your body or consciousness partly occupied by another spirit or entity, who then communicates through you.

This can sound scary and similar to possession so I completely understand why people are nervous when they first start witnessing or experiencing it.

Brett has trained in channeling. He only sort of remembers part of what he said during those training sessions, or more precisely, what was said through him. Channeling did not happen spontaneously, however. If this had been the first thing that showed up when his psychic abilities were developing we probably would have been terrified. But since it was our choice, we chalk it up as just another one of his tools. And I will admit it is certainly not his preferred method.

You may be wondering how one can be sure that:
- The spirits who enter a body will leave?
- The spirits can't make you harm yourself or others?
- You're not going to be possessed while in that condition?

The only answers I have for you are that confidence and understanding come with experience and that humans do actually have dominion over their bodies and souls. But whereas most psychic abilities can be developed independently if one prefers, I feel that channeling is the one skill that warrants finding a teacher in all cases, just to make sure you learn the techniques and types of self-protection that ensure minimal disruption to your life.

How to: For the reason mentioned above, I am going to skip instructions for channeling. I feel it's not a good idea to experiment with this skill on your own and adequate guidance is beyond the scope of this book.

The Clairs: The "clair" labels used to intimidate me and struck me as pretentious throwbacks to the Victorian era, when spiritualism was all the rage. However, if we just consider them exercises in morphology, they start to make sense.

"Clair" is based on the French word for "clear," then each of the five senses are represented by adding on Latin-based terminology. A "sixth sense" is included, which basically just refers to "knowing."

Psychics and mediums sometimes do "just know" the information they're seeking but much of the time they are receiving those messages through palpable reactions with their five sense. Either way, some form of the clairs is the basis for almost all psychic impressions.

- ***Clairvoyance:*** People with this skill can "see things clearly." So let's take a moment to discuss what psychics mean when they say they "see" something.

    Picture what you had for lunch or what you want to have for dinner. A loved one's face smiling at you during a happy time. Your favorite scene from a movie. Basically, picture any event or memory that holds significance for you. Can you "see" those things in your mind? This is often how clairvoyants or psychics see things—not as images that appear externally in the environment around them.

(Although that does happen frequently for a minority of people and on rare occasion for many others.)

If an apparition is visible to more than one person, it's likely that what you're seeing is a physical manifestation and therefore isn't necessarily clairvoyance.

"How do they know it's not just their own thought, idea, or memory?" you might ask. Fair question. It's partly a matter of trust and setting your intention to get accurate results. But also, with practice and validation, one gradually learns the subtle differences between their own thoughts and those of others.

Learning discernment and truly trusting the process are the major keys to success with any psychic ability. But at first, as long as you or others aren't relying on your psychic information, just go with it and believe that you're getting psychic impressions when you're practicing. Embracing the concept is an important part of the growth process.

- *Clairaudience:* Clear hearing. Most clairaudients hear words in their head, much like you might be able to conjure up your favorite song right now. They might hear it in their own voice, like talking to themselves, or in another's voice with distinct differences in articulation or even an accent. This is called subjective clairaudience. There is also objective clairaudience, where the sound comes from outside of the physical body but is only audible to the psychic. Again, if more than one person can hear a sound it's likely a physical phenomenon that wouldn't be categorized as clairaudience.

These skills become easier with practice. You start to notice the subtle differences between your own thoughts and what don't seem to be your own thoughts because the tone or vocabulary isn't like yours, or the information surprises you. These are ways you can distinguish between your conscious mind's chatter and details that are coming from somewhere else.

Learning to identify who outside of yourself you're communicating with is another story. That intricate level of discernment can require years of practice.

Clairaudience is the phenomenon that can most easily be confused with schizophrenia because "hearing voices" is fundamental to both. I'll reiterate what I said in Chapter 4 about this: as long as what's coming through isn't encouraging harm to oneself or others, there's not much cause for concern, except for the degree to which the person is bothered by other people sharing the space in their head.

Negatively provocative messages might be an indicator of a mental health issue, or they might just mean that the psychic is being harassed by somebody not so nice on the other side. A lot of people are jerks and those people don't necessarily turn into sweethearts just because they left their bodies. Spirits who have made the transition through the light are almost universally positive but ghosts who stay here are still playing out their personality dynamics and dramas from the life they just left.

- *Clairsentience:* Clear feeling. This is pretty synonymous with being an **empath**. You feel emotions and sensations in your body that are clearly not your own but instead they belong to someone else, living or dead. Have you ever walked into a room and it felt uncomfortable because somebody just had a fight or argument there? That's a version of clairsentience.

I get clairsentient information when I'm reading animals sometimes so I've learned that it's important to identify and then let go of others' emotions or physical sensations. They can make us physically, mentally, or emotionally sick. At the very least they are disruptive and confusing if we're unaware of the mechanism in action. Sometimes people are mistakenly thought to have mood disorders when really, they're just absorbing and playing out others' moods without realizing what's happening. It's so important to be aware of our degree of empathy in order to maintain as much self-determination as possible.

I should mention that people can feel positive emotions of others, too. Like a contact high. So it's not all bad. But even in those cases it's a good idea to be able to identify what is your own emotion versus what is someone else's.

- *Clairalience:* Clear smelling. Sounds delightful, doesn't it? (Where's that sarcasm font when I need it?) I know a woman who can tell when a spirit is present because she smells cologne or perfume from their era. She has even learned a lot about historical fragrances because this is such a frequent occurrence.

    She's not a working psychic, by the way. She's an esthetician who just happens to be able to tell when "oldies" are around (that's what she calls them). I also met another woman recently who said, "My grandmother is here, I can smell her," even though this person claims no psychic ability at all and feels like this is just normal. More reminders that we can adjust to these out-of-the-ordinary experiences and just keep living our lives.

I also heard one psychic say she has arranged for a certain foul smell to show up when someone is lying to her. She set it with intention, just like we use intention to be grounded and protected. She is adept enough and believes this strongly enough to make it actually happen and be effective for herself. I think I'd rather go with an audio cue for that (like a buzzer or bell, or maybe a certain song), but we each have to do what works for us.

- *Clairgustance:* Clear tasting. Brett was told by another psychic a few years ago that he should be able to taste when something paranormal is present and it seems like that ability is starting to kick in for him a tiny bit here and there. I'm not so sure he's going to embrace this ability though because "yuck," right?

- *Claircognizance:* Claircognizance is similar to (or perhaps exactly the same as) what humans have referred to as intuition basically forever, only on a grander scale.

    Basically, claircognizance means that you just know stuff all of a sudden. Not from inference or previous experience, but now you just have information that you couldn't possibly know unless someone or something else put it in your brain. I think this happens to almost everybody sometimes but most people give it little consideration.

It often feels like you've instantly downloaded a chunk of information that you didn't have before. Or like you already know a lot about a person upon just meeting them. It sometimes shows up as being able to answer a question you didn't think you had the answer to but all of a sudden you have a whole cache of knowledge on the subject that can't be explained.

This is perhaps the hardest modality to trust because there aren't any "tangible" indicators you can point to when trying to convince yourself or others.

Also see my write up on **intuitive/sensitive.**

How to: If you want to use these skills intentionally and not just spontaneously, first decide what kinds of information or answers you want from your Spirit Guides or whomever else might be hanging around to help you out. Then get yourself into psychic readiness mode. Make sure to use intention and psychic protection to only connect with positive, supportive entities.

Now ask your first question in your mind or aloud and then maintain your receptivity and trust that an answer will come.

You'll need to be highly aware of your body and thoughts. Are you feeling or sensing something that can't be easily explained? For example, did you get a sharp pain in your chest for a moment, or are you suddenly sad without any identifiable cause in your own life? Did new ideas or information pop into your head? Do you smell freshly baked cookies when there aren't any around? Do you all of a sudden feel like you "just know" the answer to the question when you didn't before? Did it sound like someone spoke either inside your head or right outside of your ear? Do you have a visual image in your mind that doesn't relate to your personal experience or memories? Those are the answers you're looking for. Trust them.

Not everyone receives in all of the clair forms. We each have a unique configuration of these skills. But the key is that you pay attention to what does come up and then suspend doubt about it being a message from someone else (or your Higher Self).

Smells, symbolism, and bodily sensations are sometimes vague or mysterious so you might have to spend some time decoding what you get, but just recognizing that you received any impressions at all is the first big step. With practice, the messages will get clearer, stronger, and more detailed. You will become more confident in your ability to open that line of communication when you want it and to distinguish what is your own thought from what is coming from somewhere else.

Dowsing/divining—also described in Chapter 7: When I was about 10 years old, my grandfather taught me how to use dowsing rods to find water on his property. This is my first memory of anyone in my family believing in something unexplainable or esoteric, though he certainly didn't think of it that way. He was just an old cowboy using old cowboy tools.

I don't know whether dowsing instruments like pendulums and rods operate from psychomotor effect (our subconscious receiving information and translating it to corresponding muscle activity) or whether an outside force is acting upon the tools to move them. Many people have strong opinions but I am thoroughly undecided at this point. For me, it's like every other psychic ability in that it's functionally irrelevant how it works as long as it does. And I know I can get pretty solid answers from outside of my conscious awareness with these tools so that's good enough for me.

How to: I was taught these methods without any kind of psychic readiness prep so I don't consider it necessary, but you do have to maintain the elements of intending to be successful and being willing to accept the answers you receive.

For dowsing, hold the handles or short parts of the L rods (or forked ends of the Y on the single rod) in front of you, with the functioning end(s) pointed away from your body. Hold them loosely enough that a minor force can change their direction but not so loosely that they are flopping around. Identify what you're looking for and then move around the area.

If you're holding the rods correctly they will stay fairly still until you get a response to your question. Keep your target in mind. Don't let yourself get too distracted. But otherwise it should just happen when you've hit your mark. The L-shaped rods will cross or swing apart, the Y-shaped rod will move up or down.

Pendulums are useful for more precision work or for getting binary (e.g. yes/no) answers. You use one by holding it still (aka neutral position) and then posing a question, at which time it should move in the particular motion that represents the correct answer. When you first start using a pendulum you'll want to ask it to show you "yes" and "no" so you know what to look for.

Occasionally, with my pendulum, if I want the result to be extra clear, I'll actually draw circles in opposite directions, or perpendicular lines (like x-y axis) and then label to the two distinct images "A" and "B" or "yes" and "no." This means I'm programming the pendulum for what type of answer to give me. In these cases, I'm not going to settle for just any swing but will wait until I get a response more precisely aligned with my drawing.

If you're trying to find a spot on a map or body, the indication might just be any movement at all when it reaches the correct point, if you've kept the pendulum properly still as you hover it over the image.

Because pendulums and dowsing rods have to be held by us in order to work, you'll need to be careful that you're not making it react by your own subtle movement. Sometimes it will be obvious if this is happening, but sometimes it will be ideomotor effect (like I described in the section on Ouija boards).

With practice you can overcome the tendency to unduly influence your tools and you'll become more confident that you can trust your results. This is a normal learning process so just give it a little time and you'll get the hang of it.

Empath: Synonymous with **clairsentience.** Being an empath (feeling others' feelings) has become pretty widely accepted in our society now. In fact, it seems almost ordinary at this point to know someone who is strongly affected by the sadness, happiness, nervousness, or physical discomfort of someone else in the room, just from being near them.

I would go so far as to say that short of having issues that interfere with a normal level of compassion (e.g. sociopathy or misfiring mirror neurons), we all have this sensitivity to some degree whether we realize it or not.

Empathy in children often presents as anxiety, distraction, or seemingly defiant behavior like school avoidance. Kids lack the self-awareness and vocabulary to connect their symptoms to the real cause of their discomfort, and are therefore often misdiagnosed and even medicated.

Fortunately, most adults who are hypersensitive to the people around them have an easier time explaining what's going on and have the frustration tolerance to cope with it. But you can expect a lot of the same outward behaviors or symptoms, at least in the beginning: anxiety, distraction, and avoidance of social situations.

Fortunately, with the right support they can learn ways to protect themselves and life can return to normal reasonably quickly.

How to: Empathic sensitivity is largely a passive process. Sort of like feeling the heat or coldness in a room. However, it can be amplified by paying attention to one's physical and emotional reactions when it starts happening. Sometimes by setting the intention of being more open and receptive, an empath can pick up more of the subtle energies around them. Or they can visualize a cord running from them to the other person, to see if that amplifies any impressions they get. If you choose to connect yourself to someone else, be sure to cut the cord when you're done, as discussed in Chapter 6.

ESP (Extra Sensory Perception): This is not a distinct skill but just a general term covering most of what we're talking about in this chapter. **Psi** is another term that's used to refer to paranormal and other anomalous phenomena in a general way.

Healing: First, some common-sense comments and disclaimers.

While energy healing can be powerful and can indeed eliminate many physical problems, it is imperative that clients receive standard medical attention for any issues/ailments they are experiencing. Energetic and psychic healing should be considered supplementary to treatment by a medical doctor. Energy healers need to insist upon this and should not diagnose their clients' illnesses.

One reason for this decree is the potential legal liability involved, but another is how delicate the subject of a person's health can be.

An energy healer needs to be careful about alarming someone with their comments but also needs to not gloss over any potentially problematic areas.

So for example, it's OK to say, "The energy in your chest seems heavy or unbalanced," but you shouldn't make the leap from there to saying, "You must have a problem with your heart." That would be a premature assumption and could cause the client undue distress. It's a fine line, but one that is critically important to not overstep. For both the client's sake and the healer's.

Essentially, until an energy worker has been thoroughly trained, they should avoid potential legal and personal issues by working only on cooperative family members.

OK, lecture over. Let's get on to the more interesting stuff.

When I talk about "healing" I am referring to all kinds of energetic or psychic healing. Some practitioners do it by actually laying their hands on a patient, while others can heal just as effectively from a distance. Some healers have learned a specific protocol, like Reiki, and others just figure out their own techniques or are guided by the other side. But all of the healers I know state that they are not actually doing the healing, rather that healing is being done through them.

This may be one of the more difficult abilities to accept and I'm sorry I can't tell you how it works, only that it does. My first personal experience was at just 7 years old, when a woman I'd never seen before could somehow tell I was in pain and approached me with an offer to "take my headache away." I didn't understand what she even meant but I agreed, and when she placed her hand on the side of my head I could feel the headache being sucked out of my head, like a liquid. I'd never heard of anything like that before and although it made a big impression at the time, it didn't cross my mind again until I was trying to find examples for this section.

A more recent personal instance involves Brett's healing ability. I have on my medical record a condition called eosinophilic esophagitis that causes my esophagus to completely close up. My trigger food was potatoes. I say "was" because with a single session, Brett eradicated my potato issue, for which I had been scoped, officially diagnosed, and told there was no known cure or even temporary relief of symptoms.

You may say, "Well that was just psychosomatic," which is a completely legitimate assertion when a person knows they're being worked on.

There's been much research over the past few years about the mystery that is the placebo effect. The medical industry has demonstrated that it works even when patients know they're getting a placebo. So if your partner can eliminate symptoms or pain from people's lives simply by convincing them that they're better, that still qualifies as healing because it's what happens a lot in traditional medicine, too. The mind-body connection is a powerful force.

However, most recipients of healing energy say they feel warmth or vibration when the work is being done. And the fact that conditions can sometimes be improved even when a patient doesn't know they're being worked on points to a legitimate process happening.

When Brett worked on me I was standing in a doorway with my eyes closed. I could feel sensations in my chest but I couldn't see what he was doing. At a certain point I lost my balance because it felt like I was being pushed, even though he wasn't touching me. And then voilà, no more potato problem. He didn't know what he'd worked on, only that he was feeling compelled to move energy into and out of my chest. It was only later that we realized the result, when I didn't have a reaction to trace amounts of potato in my food one day.

Healing is one of those abilities that can easily cause grandiosity if it comes on suddenly and spontaneously. (Grandiosity is less likely if the person has chosen to develop the skill through diligent practice.) They say that some doctors have a "God complex" because they can save people's lives, but what if you could make people better without any tools or medicine? What if sometimes your mere presence actually had a healing effect on people? Talk about a God complex.

There is a related category of psychics called *medical intuitives*. These people are able to identify or diagnose medical issues but they haven't developed healing skills or for some reason choose not to use them.

Unfortunately, even the best healers can't always fix everything. That's important for us to remember both as patients and as practitioners.

Healers take away energy that isn't supposed to be there and as much as we would like to think that every ailment, malady, disease, disorder, or discomfort isn't supposed to be part of our lives, from a spiritual perspective that just isn't true. Some hardships are challenges we agreed to before being born, in order to grow spiritually. Some people may call it the cycle of karma and I'd be OK with that explanation (though I stay away from the idea of karma as punishment).

The point is that not all pain or suffering is meant to be alleviated, as much as we would like it to be. Or at least not without any effort or lifestyle change on our part.

Here's a list of a few energy healing techniques that have received widespread recognition. This list is by no means exhaustive, it's just a taste. It's important to know that many natural-born healers don't necessarily use any standardized technique and instead just develop their own skills organically. But others choose to study a program with a proven track record or high name recognition. As with everything else, it's just a choice each person makes. One way is not better than the other. But perhaps looking into some of these techniques will help you better understand where your partner's natural talents lie.

- *CHIOS*
- *EFT®--Emotional Freedom Techniques*
- *Healing Touch*
- *Polarity Therapy*
- *Pranic Healing*
- *Quantum Touch®*
- *Reiki*
- *Shamanic Healing*

Proficiency with healing methods is obtainable for *everyone*, not just people who have already noticed an inherent ability for healing. But you knew I was going to say that.

Even without committing to the serious training of a tried-and-true program like the ones above, you can start to work with energy/psychic healing on your own. Your self-taught skills may not be as strong or as broadly applicable, but everyone has at least a rudimentary capacity for energy work. We are beings of energy (remember auras?) so it really only makes sense that we can train ourselves to be more aware of energy and to use it in a conscious fashion.

How to: Energy work is a practice that calls for psychic readiness. Be sure you're protecting yourself very well and also setting the intention to not take on anyone else's issues by working with them. At the end you'll want to cut cords and cleanse yourself in some way, and make sure you haven't absorbed any energy from the client.

A main component of energy work is envisioning that it's happening and setting the intention for it to happen (and for you to be able to sense it).

There are so many approaches that have specific protocols and many call for first trying to sense the energy between your own hands. Personally, I can seldom feel the energy between my hands and that used to bother me but it doesn't anymore. I just trust that whatever I'm supposed to do will happen.

When I try energy work I tend to actually lay my hands on Brett or my dogs, but it's not necessary and in fact, many people say it's actually better to hover your hands a few inches away from the body instead of making contact. I say do whatever feels the most effective to you, unless you're learning a specific technique and then definitely follow their directions.

However, before touching a client you must always get their permission. Always. And there are different thoughts on whether it's OK to work on children at all, which brings up a higher-level philosophical discussion about free will and soul growth that I will save for another book. But I'd suggest that healers refrain from working on anyone under 18 until this issue is thoroughly considered (except their own children, of course).

Once you're in readiness mode and are in proximity to your subject, send light/energy from your hands to the client. You may not feel anything but keep doing it anyway. If all you can do is envision it at this point, do so with detail. See it entering the body or cascading over the skin, or whatever you want it to do.

If it helps intensify your vision to be specific, you can imagine energy coming from the atmosphere or down from the sky, through the back of your hands and out of your palms.

Whomever you're working on, even if it's an animal, you may notice that they twitch where you're sending energy. Or they might yawn. Dogs and horses might do what is called "lick and chew"—that thing they do with their tongue that seems like they're trying to get peanut butter off the roof of their mouth. These are all very good signs. It means that they're consciously or subconsciously registering changes in their energy based on your work.

The validation of seeing someone react is exciting and encouraging, but just because you don't notice a physical reaction, don't assume that nothing is happening. People have varying degrees of body and energy awareness. If they don't show a physical response, they might report what they sensed or felt after the fact. But even if they can't identify anything at all, just continue to trust and practice.

Once you're seeing/feeling the energy penetrate through the body, look for black holes that need to be filled up with light/energy, or black gunk that needs to be blasted out by it. Sometimes a blockage will deflect the energy away, which just lets you know that area needs extra work.

Conversely, sometimes stuck or negative energy needs to be pulled out of the body. I'm sure there are as many techniques for this as there are healers, but one visualization I use is that I'm wearing a magnetic glove and the "bad stuff" in the body is like metal shavings that are easily attracted.

If you pull energy out of someone like this, be sure you've set up a mechanism through intention for safely disposing of what you draw out. You can purify your glove or hand in a shower of white light, for example. I take the psychic glove off and throw it into an imagined fireplace.

Yes, all of this is driven by visualization. So much of healing work takes place on that level. Ideally, both you and your subject will have had visceral experiences like feeling energy or heat or twitching while you're working on them. And of course you'll want to see tangible results of improvement in their condition afterward (though maybe not immediately because bodies take a while to adjust) to build your confidence. But the process of figuring out where the energy needs to go is largely accomplished through your mind's eye and intuition.

I've given you just enough to play around with it but if you're serious about developing this ability, please seek out some mentorship or training. And imagine what a great place the world would be if we could all affect even just a small amount of healing on each other. Removing aches and pains or the beginning stages of common illnesses. This is one skill that is definitely worth trying out.

Intuitive/sensitive (aka claircognizant): It's when you just know something. Like thinking that someone is going to call and then the phone rings. Or how parents frequently have gut feelings when their children are in trouble, without any explanation for why they would know that.

These are the kind of intuitive hits that everyone gets. They're considered commonplace and normal. Cops value this type of extrasensory awareness so much that they even have a name for it: "blue sense." Their hunches and instincts help keep them alive in volatile situations and sometimes contribute to them solving cases.

Like all of *the Clairs* and basically every other category of psychic, the intuitive has to learn to distinguish between their own thoughts, feelings, and sensory experiences and those coming from outside sources. Again, it comes down to discernment and paying attention.

By now you can start to see how all of these categories overlap and depend upon interpretation. Is she a "clairvoyant empath" or is she an "intuitive" who hears and feels things on a subtle level? My opinion is that most of the time, labeling is really just an economizing of words or a shorthand so people can easily get the gist of what you're talking about without having to explain it from the beginning every time.

And in the case of novices, labels help by giving a starting point for further research.

How to: Sensitivity or intuition generally describes an ability to passively receive information. However, like empathy, it can be enhanced by your willingness to receive and accept what you're getting. By being a conscious and willing participant, so to speak, you can start to feel more confident about the content and reliability of what you pick up.

Mediumship: It figures that right after I make a deal about labels being ambiguous I come to one that isn't. Mediumship specifically means being a "medium of communication" between the living and the dead (or an entity in another dimension). As always, the methods people use to do this are widely varied, but to be a medium means this one specific thing when using the term correctly.

But while there is a huge difference between mediumship and other types of psychic ability by definition, there isn't necessarily a huge difference functionally. Some mediums actually see spirits "objectively" (outside of themselves) and others see them subjectively (in their mind's eye). Most of a medium's input comes through their strongest modalities (or *clairs*), the same way it does for other types of psychics.

How to: Naturally proficient mediums often don't have to prepare or make a conscious effort to initiate contact. As you may have seen on TV shows, some people are being constantly pestered by spirits who want to pass messages on to their loved ones who are still living.

But if you want to try mediumship without this innate ability, start with your psychic readiness prep. In this case, be sure to be clear about who you're open to talking to. If you're too eager and willing to talk to "anyone," you make yourself vulnerable to a wide range of nasty personalities and entities.

It's also better to have established a relationship with your Spirit Guides so they can act as gatekeepers during your mediumship sessions. If you have not done this previously, at the very least, now ask that they assist you in this process and not let anybody negative through.

Once you're truly in a quiet and receptive state of mind, and have done due diligence with your psychic protection, you can ask whether there are any spirits who would like to talk.

When your instinct tells you the time is right, go ahead and ask some questions and then sit quietly to receive the answers.

As always, it's a good sign when you are a little confused by the message or when it's said with words you wouldn't use. This helps give credibility to the idea that it's coming from another source.

You might also just get images, symbols, emotions, or physical sensations. These are all legitimate ways that experienced mediums get information. For now it may all seem fragmented, or you might be receiving a weak signal. That's OK, you're a beginner. You'll get better with practice.

Record your session in your journal in case you need to go back to that information later.

Now here are two important things to remember.

First, spirits are people, just not in a body anymore. So if you make a successful connection with someone, remember to treat them as well as you would another human being, face to face. Spirits are not "it," they are "he" or "she." Ghosts are not a sideshow, reacting to prompts for our amusement. They're people trying to communicate and be validated by our acknowledgement of them. Be sure to use your manners accordingly. And don't make promises you can't keep, like saying you'll pass on a message to someone's granddaughter if you have no means or intention of doing so.

Second, there are entities out there besides well-meaning, well-behaved spirits, and they will take you up on your invitation to talk just as readily as the nice people you probably meant to be calling. That's why psychic protection is so important. If at any time you feel uncomfortable or unsafe, shut yourself down, ask your Spirit Guides or Higher Power to intervene, and tell all spirits to leave. Put up a barrier. Do whatever you need to do to cut off contact with whatever came through that door you opened. (And yes, sometimes it is a "what" and not a "who.")

Precognition: If you think about the prefix and root of this word you naturally come to a definition like "knowing before," right? That's exactly what precognition is. This is what so many people think when they hear the word "psychic." They assume it means someone can predict the future. (And they desperately hope it means someone can predict the future results of the lottery but the Universe doesn't seem to have it set up that way for most of us.)

Each precognitor gets input through their own unique combination of all the modes, methods, and techniques that we've discussed in other sections. But most people get premonitions or precognitive messages randomly, which can be upsetting or frustrating because they don't necessarily have the specifics like a time or location reference to make the information useful.

I have two personal experiences of precognition from my adolescence. When I was around 13, I had a strong, unsettling vision of a big party at my aunt's house. Everyone was a little older, but one of my cousins wasn't there. I explained it to my mom and kept saying, "But I can't find Sarah! I can't find Sarah."

She assured me it was probably just my imagination but that if there was really such a party in future, Sarah was probably at a friend's house or there would be some other mundane reason I didn't see her there.

Very unfortunately, my little cousin Sarah died five years later. She was still in elementary school. When I walked into my aunt's house for the wake I saw the exact scene from my vision. My mother pointed out that it wouldn't serve any purpose to tell my family so besides her and Brett, this is the first time anyone is hearing about it. But I'm glad I'd told her about it when the vision originally happened so I had someone to verify that I'd really had a premonition.

The other wasn't so significant. Again in my early teens, I had a vision of looking down a hallway at two young men. One was short, one was of average height. I could see the furniture in the room and the way each was standing, and I felt myself looking fondly at them from a distance while they were unaware. At the time I thought to myself, "It must be that I'm going to have two sons!" For several years this image popped into my mind occasionally and I looked forward to it happening in real life because it was such a pleasant scene. And then one day, it did.

Turns out, they weren't my sons, they were two of my roommates in my early 20s. I stopped in the hallway one afternoon because it felt familiar, and sure enough, I saw the two of them doing exactly what I'd envisioned many years earlier. Even the lighting coming through the patio window was the same.

These visions happened long before I'd given up my stance as an atheist, before I acknowledged that there was any validity to this kind of phenomenon on a universal scale. But even though I couldn't explain it with my worldview at the time, I had no doubt that I actually "predicted the future" with my two premonitions.

This kind of unintentional viewing of the future is how most precognition works. The **remote viewing** community, however, has developed successful protocols for intentionally seeking out targeted information about other times and places, including the future. Please see the RV section for more information.

How to: When we have these spontaneous precognitive visions during waking hours, they usually feel more significant than the rest of the endless stream of random images that are constantly filling our heads. That's why it's easy to remember them, even years later.

If you want to have more confirmation or validation than just trusting your own memory, tell someone you're close to and/or write it in your new journal with all the details you can remember and be sure to record the date. By letting the Universe know that you are interested in having these experiences, you may increase their frequency.

Some people choose to pursue training in precognitive dreaming because it's a modality of psychic ability that is more understandable or more palatable for them. Enter into your sleep state with the explicit intentions to receive premonitions through your dreams and also to remember your dreams. Record every possible detail in your journal so you can learn to identify what is literal and what is symbolic.

Eventually you will start to recognize useful information that is given to you that previously would have seemed random and pointless. You can even ask for guidance about certain situations or ask to see future events. For most people, learning to use your dreams for a purpose is a gradual process that requires perseverance.

Psychography (automatic writing): To me, the term automatic writing actually describes a spectrum of related phenomena instead of just one process. All of them involve writing (or we could extrapolate to include other art forms such as painting) that happens not from one's own conscious effort but from being in "the flow."

This flow might just be tapping into your Higher Self. It might be inspired by Guides or spirits, allowing you to write in a manner distinct from your typical style. Or in rare cases another entity might actually have physical control of your hand to spell out the words. All of these qualify.

How to: I personally like to use a version of automatic writing to tap into my subconscious. The process is simple: Write your questions with your dominant hand, then let the answers flow with your non-dominant hand. It seems like you'd just get your usual answers only messier, but it's interesting to see how different the responses turn out to be.

In order to try to have someone else write through you, get yourself into psychic readiness, then be clear about who you would like to come through. (Remember my warning about mediumship: there are plenty of beings—human and otherwise—who are not so nice and will swoop in when the door is open if you don't set your boundaries and intentions right.)

It often helps to have a question or topic of conversation figured out before you start, but sometimes making the invitation to fill a blank page will be enough.

While writing, don't stop. Don't correct or judge. As much as possible, don't even consider what you're putting on the page. Just let your hand move and keep moving.

When you're done, when there doesn't seem to be any more information coming through, then you can go back over it and see what messages you got.

If it sounds out of character or talks about things you don't understand—good! That means you were possibly tapping into somebody outside of yourself (or at least outside of your conscious self). It should ideally sound like someone else was talking.

You can also do this by typing on your keyboard but I know for myself, I'm less likely to judge or correct what's coming through me if I'm writing with pen on paper. I specifically prefer the feel of a ballpoint pen when doing automatic writing even though in other cases I prefer a gel pen. Play around until you figure out your own perfect combo.

Psychometry: Psychometry is the ability to know things about the owner or history of an object by touching it. One common practical application is that psychic investigators use it to help tune in to the victim or alleged perpetrator of a crime so they can share information that police detectives might use in a criminal investigation.

How to: Get into psychic readiness mode. Have a friend give you a mystery object. Pick it up, or touch it if it's too big to pick up, and begin to connect with it. Try to shift your consciousness to that item. This means to feel like you're focusing only on that item and letting all other thoughts and distractions go as much as possible. Actually visualize a strong energetic bond.

As soon as you connect you may start receiving thoughts, feelings, images, or words. At this point, resist the temptation to reject information that contradicts assumptions you make based on what the item looks like (e.g. old pocket watch you might assume belonged to an old man and you therefore dismiss impressions that don't seem to fit with that story) or to nudge things in the direction you think they should go. Just write down absolutely everything without judgment.

Some teachers suggest that you start saying aloud all of the information that comes to you, without doubting or editing yourself. They believe that this stream of consciousness is one of the best ways to keep that energy flowing and that you'll be right a lot more of the time than you expect.

It's most useful to do this work with items with verifiable backgrounds so you can know what you got right. Once you feel like you "get it," there is value in starting to work with random pieces to see if you can feel the energy bond and develop ease with your unique flow of information. Remember, when you're surprised or doubtful about what you're getting, that's often when it's most correct.

Remote viewing: The movie *The Men Who Stare at Goats* was Hollywood's quasi-comedic portrayal of a real U.S. Army program called Project Star Gate, where soldiers were trained to be "psychic spies." The program was reportedly shut down in the mid-'90s but I know RVers still consult operationally for the military so take the phrase "shut down" for what you will.

Remote viewing is literally just that: viewing things remotely. The target can be in the present, past, or future. The military applications of being able to locate and describe a distant location or impending event are obvious. There are also countless uses for this modality in the business world and even for personal benefit.

Many psychics can achieve this result naturally, but the military spent time and money developing training protocols for people who feel they have no innate psychic ability. In fact, the military program reported better results from people who didn't identify as psychic because they were a blank slate.

To my (initial) surprise, during the trainings and practice sessions I've participated in, there has never been a single person who couldn't do remote viewing. Even total beginners. So even if you don't feel you can do other psychic stuff, you can definitely do this.

Remote viewing is now widely used around the world in its original form and people are also constantly adapting those military protocols for efficiency and use in different practical and fun scenarios. Associative Remote Viewing, Controlled Remote

Viewing, Coordinate Remote Viewing, Extended Remote Viewing. I know a guy who created a variation to predict horse races. And there are many others. Some are rigorous even in how you record the information you see during your session but others are flexible and emphasize figuring out each viewer's unique style for arriving at the right answer.

But all of them are based on this basic format: Someone chooses a target and another person tries to view and describe that target without any previous knowledge about it. That is remote viewing in a nutshell.

How to: Instructions for true, pure remote viewing in its original form are beyond the scope of this book. But I will summarize the main elements so you have a basic understanding.

You're going to need a partner for this because you need to have someone else select your target and keep it secret until you're done. There's always one or more layers of separation between the remote viewer and the knowledge of what is being viewed. This is an essential element of all forms of RV.

RVers use a process similar to what we're calling psychic readiness only they call it a "cool down." Same idea. Clearing your mind, setting your intention to be successful, etc.

Once you're ready, focus on the "coordinate" or "tasking." This terminology refers to the random number assigned by your partner to represent their secret predetermined location or answer of interest. An RV coordinate does not correlate to geographical coordinates, just to be clear. It's usually just a set of numbers made up by a person or a random number generator.

As the viewer you are charged with one task: describe the designated target. That usually includes drawing and also written verbal description. Sights, sounds, visceral feelings. Do you feel cold suddenly for no reason? Are you hearing a children's nursery rhyme? Do you feel like there's light shining in your eyes? You should include that information. Include everything you come up with, even if it doesn't make logical sense.

The written/drawn results of your remote viewing session are called a "transcript." You and/or your partner judge your transcript against the target they selected to see what you got right and what you got wrong. When you do this quite a bit you start to notice the patterns that are unique to your brain, and it helps interpret future information more effectively.

In real-world (or "operational") settings, however, viewers are often not told what the target was or what they got wrong and right. This happens a lot for RVers who work with law enforcement. They almost never get to know whether the information they provided was useful or how the investigation turned out.

Telekinesis (aka psychokinesis or "pk" for short): Moving things with your mind.

"Do not try and bend the spoon, that's impossible. Instead, only try to realize the truth: there is no spoon."

This is what a wise little boy tells Keanu Reeves in *The Matrix*. Mention of telekinesis always makes me think of that scene now because though I have never witnessed Force-like telekinesis, where something is floated around by sheer thought power, once I was able to bend a spoon and fork. It was at a "spoon bending party," full of physicists and engineers who were curious about the flip side of reality as being revealed through quantum mechanics. A cold fusion scientist with lots of success with spoon bending (and who reports having seen a convincing, mind-blowing telekinesis demonstration himself in Japan) led our group in the process. At least 90% of the people in the room were able to do it. As you can imagine, that ranks among the most fun parties I have ever attended.

I have also witnessed physical items moving without anyone touching them, but this has always been the work of somebody or something in another dimension. By this I mean mostly ghosts, which would then be considered poltergeist activity and not telekinesis, since the movement wasn't the result of a living human affecting an item with their mind or will. (Exciting or scary, yes. Telekinesis, no.)

Expect it to take much longer to get demonstrable results with telekinesis than basically any other psychic ability because most other modalities require you only to tap into the energetic flow of the Universe, whereas telekinesis requires you to manipulate it. Some teachers say it may take years of practice to begin to see results.

Because of the really long learning curve for this skill, it is perhaps not the best one to try first, or at the very least should not be the only ability you're trying to develop. To get no results for a long time can be discouraging, so work with other modalities besides telekinesis so you don't lose hope and motivation. Healing practices, for example, can offer much quicker validation that something is actually happening on an energetic level.

Other commonly mentioned caveats are that you must absolutely believe that telekinesis is possible in general and specifically for yourself, and you must also accept the theory that we are not as separate from our surroundings as we typically assume.

Universal energy is flowing through us and also through everything else, even inanimate objects. When we talk about energy in this context, don't think of it as relating only to what is alive and moving. Think of it more as the mysterious stuff that is all-pervasive in the Universe on a quantum level. Understanding that moving or changing an item is possible because we are connecting to it on an energetic level is absolutely foundational. In fact, accepting on a profound level that we are actually "one with the object" is more accurate.

How to: Once you've truly embraced the ideas about Universal energy and your ability to affect objects with your mind, you can begin practicing telekinesis by getting into psychic readiness mode.

Then start with small items. Don't start with large goals, keep it simple. Try to make a candle flame react in a specific way. Realize that it's in a purely energetic form already so you don't have to manipulate anything as dense as matter to make this work.

Visualize what you want the flame to do. Remind yourself that you and the flame are made of the same energy and that it's flowing between you. See yourself as part of the same pool of energy as the flame and everything else around you.

The process is the same no matter what your target is. Maintain your mindset of psychic readiness and hold onto the idea that you and the item are one energetic system. Remain focused, relaxed, and undistracted. Tension, frustration, self-doubt, and distraction will all break your connection with the object. Then use visualization to guide your mutual energy in your desired manner.

Telepathy: Being able to read another's thoughts or project your thoughts into someone else's mind. I mentioned telepathy briefly in the beginning of Chapter 8. This, like precognition, is one of the things people might assume you mean when you say you're psychic unless you go into further detail.

Even though I still contend that no one can breach your mind in a significant fashion, I do believe that telepathy happens to everyone on a low level all the time whether they realize it or not.

When we first got together we used to be amazed by how often one of us would think of something random and the other would say it out loud just a few moments later, or we would have the same thought at the same time even though we were miles apart and we'd send simultaneous emails about it. Now it's so commonplace that we rarely mention it except in jest to see who should get credit for a good idea.

When a seemingly random idea pops into your mind and your loved one is around, find out if they were just thinking about that same thing. You might be pleasantly surprised to see how linked you really are on a deeper level. It's kind of fun.

A lot of ideas we assume are due to our brains going on tangents are actually thoughts received from loved ones, our animals, coworkers, and even strangers we happen to be standing near. It's a testament to how detached we've become from our basic natures that we don't realize these connections are happening and that we don't tend to cultivate them intentionally.

As I mentioned earlier, telepathy is how I work with animals. They use it amongst themselves extensively and can read our minds regardless of proximity. I bring this up again only to point out the importance of being mindful with our thoughts. Isn't the fact that they can impact the people and animals around us a reason to improve the quality of what we have going on up there?

How to: There are lots of opportunities to practice telepathy spontaneously, like trying to figure out why a person is calling before you answer the phone. But if you want to practice in a more intentional manner, start by finding a partner, then both of you should grab a pen and paper and get into psychic readiness mode.

Someone will be the sender and someone will be the receiver. When you're both ready, the sender should imagine a fairly basic object and hold that image strongly in their mind. If they can manage to visualize floating the image to the receiver's mind, even better, but it can work without this step.

As the receiver, make a mental note about (or preferably, write down) the impressions you're getting in your empty mind. Don't be frustrated by the fact that you may get associations or characteristics instead of seeing an exact object. This is very common. Part of being a professional or accomplished psychic is learning to interpret what comes through symbolically or in pieces because not everything is 100% intact and clear all the time.

In my first attempt with a stranger at an Intro to Animal Communication workshop, one detail I got was "pink angora sweater." My partner imagined a pink bunny, which isn't a naturally occurring thing, so my mind went a step off target. But I wrote down specifically "pink angora sweater" not just "pink sweater" so we considered that a hit in terms of me actually catching the signal she was sending about the bunny. That's why it's important to record every detail that comes up. Sometimes the seemingly trivial parts are what will give you the most validation.

After you do this exercise, switch sender and receiver roles. It will help you learn the process better by being on both sides of the equation and it will also help drive home how anyone can be psychic.

Gradually, you can increase the complexity of imagery or you can start guessing what card will come up next in the deck, etc. Maybe you can even influence what your significant other brings home for dinner by putting the idea of what you want in their mind.

***

The advice in this book is a lot to take in all at once. Don't feel like you should have this situation mastered already. Just start with the basics:

- Be your partner's #1 fan. Always.
- Keep an open mind (even when it's hard).
- Maintain the infrastructure of your life so each challenge feels like a molehill, not a mountain.
- Still do the things that make you happy.
- Get support if it will help.

Everything else is icing on the cake. (Really delicious icing.)

When it comes to metaphysics, the more knowledgeable and accepting you are, the richer and more exciting your life will be. So many of us have wished we had The Force or could wield genuine magic or perform miracles, and now in a sense we can, if we embrace the unique permutations of psychic or healing ability that seem to be awakening.

But even if you don't want that right now and you're just focused on bringing balance back to your relationship, the guidelines I've laid out in this book can get you there. Incorporate as many as you can into your daily dealings with your significant other. The increased sense of closeness and stability will be palpable.

Chapter 10

DON'T JUST TAKE MY WORD FOR IT

I've talked enough about what has worked for me, as someone who has successfully supported a partner through a significant period of transformation (and has benefited greatly from the process herself). Let's wrap up with some firsthand accounts and opinions from mediums, energy healers, psychics, and everyday empaths.

I solicited this mostly anonymous input from friends and casual acquaintances and even one family member who I found out has "skills" only after I started asking around. None of the respondents had read a single word of what I'd written before giving me their statements. (Not even Brett.) I asked them to describe their own growth experiences and tell us what support and responses from loved ones are helpful and unhelpful. These are the spontaneous, very personal messages they wanted to share with you.

Brett Carstens

When I met Crystal I had already been having strange paranormal experiences for most of my life. I saw ghosts regularly when I was a kid and from that point I sought out experiences that affirmed that the world was a much larger, more wondrous and magical place than we typically perceive. She quickly accepted and appreciated my open mind and viewpoint, even with her limited personal experiences at that time.

Without that acceptance, our relationship wouldn't have been able to develop and grow how it has over the past fifteen or so years. Her open mind allowed me to feel free to express mine and I think, allowed her to start having some paranormal experiences herself.

Now, I'm not saying that she was seeking it out. It seemed to scare her at first, and some of her first encounters weren't all that pleasant, like the time she was choked by a jealous ghost at the Plaza Hotel in Las Vegas. But eventually she came around and was able to accept that what was happening on that level was real.

As I began to develop my psychic abilities and go through a spiritual awakening, she was already primed to be able to help me with the transition. And it *is* a major transition. My paradigm shifted so much that even I, Mr. Open Minded, could hardly keep up. But she was there to support me in what I was going through.

I know that she suspended disbelief as I began to see and communicate with unseen beings, but she never let on or even hinted at not believing in what I claimed to be experiencing. It was difficult enough for me to trust my own senses because many of these phenomena are so outside of our perception and the emphasis on physical-world reality that most of us grow up with. But I needed to trust it so I could continue to develop and not just assume I was crazy. If she had doubted me, I would have doubted myself and who knows how things would have turned out.

She's also been a proponent of my development, encouraging me to pursue my passion, talk about it, and keep her in the loop. She listens and then helps me reason out what's occurred, giving me another angle on it. When it gets too deep or scary, she's been there to inject some humor into the situation, or even find something to distract me to pull me back to the "real" world. And, I'm grateful to have had her there to validate my earliest experiences.

Having a partner who shows that she believes in me and what I'm experiencing, who's willing to go along for the ride, to grow with me, and help me ground through humor and distraction when necessary, has been invaluable to my spiritual and psychic development.

***

I can see, hear, and speak with spirits. My gift started with seeing them when I was 7, which evolved into hearing their stories and then beyond. I have learned to listen to their advice and access their wisdom for my own benefit and to support the people I care about. I even have several spirits willing to help me when people ask questions.

My mother was highly supportive, for she could see spirits as well. Her side of the family never judged or doubted me. The best part was that they listened and believed me when I told them there was another person in the room, or if I sensed a person moving on.

My father, on the other hand, was skeptical, and his parents would often insult my abilities, denounce the stories I told them as "just my imagination," or call me "crazy" or "demon child."

Those sorts of things only make it worse for children/adults who have psychic abilities.

I want people to know: There is nothing to fear from the spirit realm. Scary stuff like what's shown in the movie *Paranormal Activity* feeds off negative and aggressive spirits/demons, but these do not exist everywhere. I'd say 90% of the entities in the spirit realm are positive spirits who want to help humans, not harm them. So don't worry.

***

One time, when I was around 12 years old, I was home alone having popcorn and watching a movie. I suddenly felt uncomfortable and sensed vibration, then the front door started to shake as if someone were on the other side twisting the knob violently and slamming the door back and forth in its tiny bit of wiggle room.

I was terrified. I ran out onto the balcony and hung off the edge by my hands, watching the door continue its thrashing.

I looked away for a moment to assess my options for a next move and when I looked back the door was slowly swinging open! Now I was really scared, so I dropped into the neighbor's balcony below me and made my way down to the first floor, thinking I would enter my house through the front door later. When I eventually went back home nobody was there but the door was still open.

Now as an adult I have frequent psychic/paranormal experiences, mostly through sound and feeling, and I have evolved into someone who can protect myself from energy that I am not interested in having around me. But I don't talk to my family about it. They aren't helpful in this regard. They aren't interested or open minded enough. I do share this with my extended family (godparents) and they totally get it. They've taken me to observe paranormal phenomena on more than one occasion. They also offer guidance when I ask or when they feel I am ready.

When you see or feel something you can't explain, it's no less real just because science hasn't figured it out yet. Maybe the only difference between imagination and reality is belief. I believe, so I can do things that many people can't. You just need to practice hearing, feeling, and seeing. Try and remember what it was like when you were little and everything felt like magic to you. It still is. It hasn't changed, you have.

***

I am an empath who experiences channeled messages. I also have healing ability that has been very useful for people both in my presence and far across the globe.

I took a strong interest in these matters from a young age, but was made fun of. Then I made the mistake of playing with a Ouija board at 18 and had horrible things happen. It was not until I had a vision of the astrological wheel with all the signs dancing and Hebrew letters on fire coming out of the center that I gave myself permission to really study again at age 30.

I didn't get any genuine respect from most of my loved ones until I opened the metaphysical store and gained recognition from others. I was always accused of being "too sensitive." But now I realize it was all part of the gift.

As an adult I've learned to use the mechanism that gives me helpful insights for my clients as inspiration in improvisational acting, which is very cathartic for me and audiences seem to enjoy.

Everyone has this ability and can develop with practice. It's a muscle. Some are born naturally stronger, but it is available to everyone. Just like going to the gym. And we all have a guidance crew!!

***

I was always good at sizing people up when I was little, so that part has been with me from a young age. As a teenager I started taking classes and made time to meditate, which helped answer a lot of questions and allowed me to find the insights I was seeking. Finally, around age 23 I made the commitment to pursue intuitive work as something legitimate in my life through more frequent classes and consistent practice.

My abilities generally involve being able to describe someone's personality, their physical and/or emotional state, and their environment (for example, their house), plus give information about people close to them, as well as knowing their memories and perhaps something that is or was important to them. I can also feel, hear, or see their struggles. Stuff like that. I usually get these impressions whether I am in the same room with them or we're on the phone.

My goal is to let people know they are not alone by giving them evidence (messages and such) that spirits and entities on the other side are helping them.

Fortunately, my parents have been supportive. My dad has some mild interest in intuition and it runs in the family on my mom's side. They helped pay for classes when I was younger and generally supported whatever I was drawn to learning.

My friends' reactions have ranged from being curious to not believing to not liking the idea at all. Friends or family that don't ask me about my work and avoid the subject totally bum me out, but sometimes it's even worse. One of my best friends, this work clashes with her religious beliefs so we don't talk as much as we used to, which makes me sad. Another friend told me they have to keep their family away from me due to how I have chosen to live my life, and I had a family member say that my line of work is just a bunch of liars and none of it is real. So I've experienced a lot of isolation, avoidance, and rejection from people I was previously close to.

My fiancé was the first person I had an extensive conversation with who was on the fence but at least considered the possibility of it being real simply because I believe in it and he believes in me. He actually learned my perspective and listened. That type of support was huge for me. And it's really cool when friends want to try out a Reiki session or reading. Their participation benefits me because I gain experience in addition to feeling supported. Some other friends have helped me with Facebook and my website.

Other than that I only have conversations with people who already love the subject, are genuinely curious, or at least want to have an intelligent skeptical debate.

I find that people who are against energy/intuitive work usually don't understand what it even means most of the time. This stuff is becoming more mainstream but can still seem esoteric and definitions can be hazy. I truly believe that everyone is capable of reading energy, you just have to have an open mind and heart.

***

I have always seen spirits and been aware of their influence. I started studying religions, myths, and magic at age 9, despite the fact that most of my family are religious fanatics who provided my young mind with a mythos that was very hard to shake free of. It's important that we all follow our hearts.

The method I've developed is to work in dreams, where I can find the answer to any question and fight or defend from spirits. And I often see future events (mundane ones) in my dreams.

I have left my body and travelled between. Additionally, I am highly empathic and can sense and influence others' emotions, including harnessing the energy from peak emotions to influence things, cause harm, etc. I also do a lot of exorcist work with the particularly nasty entities. (Trust me: Don't chase monsters, they will chase you back.)

I still don't discuss anything with my family that I think they'd see as the realm of the devil. An exception was when I started working to expand my abilities, I brought it up to my grandmother and she told me her mother-in-law was known for her abilities, too, some of which were very similar.

***

One day several years ago I was with a couple of friends who claimed to be clairvoyant. All of a sudden, both of them started reacting strongly in the direction of the window, saying that some entity was trying to get through. One left to fetch a "magic kit," leaving me and the other sensitive in the apartment, but he felt uneasy being there so we went for a walk.

All this time I was extremely skeptical and thought they were touched with high imagination. I wasn't really a big proponent of the idea that these two had powers.

Well, after the walk, we entered the apartment through the kitchen. It felt really stuffy. When we walked into the living room I noticed that room had no pressure at all. Hmm. That was unusual. I walked back into the kitchen. Higher pressure. Living room, nothing. I asked him where the little girl that supposedly haunts the apartment was. "She's in the kitchen, dude," he replied.

At that point I realized that I could sense spirits, too.

In the beginning my sensitivity was rough, but it got sharper and more refined over the years. Through research, my own insight, and working with enlightened people, I've learned to understand the ins and outs of empathy/clairsentience and how to work with energy. I now consider myself an empath, healer, spiritual guide, and teacher of psychic development, and I can remove spirits/entities.

Since I don't come from a close family I have only involved them minimally in my spiritual journey. Instead I have relied on friends who are more understanding and conversant on this subject. I kept it on the down low from everyone else for years.

My mom was skeptical at first because I had been a flighty, generally unfocused, subpar kind of guy with a supersized imagination most of my life, but she didn't put me down. She knows what I can do now and hopes I can make a living at it someday. I work with my sister and her boyfriend, helping them develop their abilities.

On the other hand, my brother doesn't really say anything and his wife is a skeptic who disagrees with my assumptions, but not to my face. They live up north so I rarely see them and I don't anticipate us resolving our differences on this matter. It hardly concerns me that they're skeptical, though. Lots of people are.

We know that the body is composed of both biological and electrical systems, and energy work/healing simply works on those systems. Thoughts have energy too, and it's pretty widely understood now that our thoughts affect our bodies the same way stress does. Plus our bodies soak up energy from a variety of sources every day. Someday, science will be able to track this.

You have to remember that science is far behind in matters of the brain and we barely understand how our minds and grey matter actually work.

Once you start to realize that modern science does not have it all figured out, you'll see how there are many things that can't be explained through the scientific method. It is the hubris we humans have that makes us believe we've conquered nature and unraveled all the secrets of the universe, but we're still making discoveries every day. Lift your skepticism a little bit and accept that there are things/subjects we as a species are still struggling to understand. "Supernatural/paranormal" phenomena are part of that collection of unknown knowledge. It's just another system waiting to be uncovered.

***

I suppose I'd describe paranormal experiences and psychic abilities as related or say that one that leads to the other. I think in order to have a paranormal experience you need to be a bit more "open" to it, maybe even somewhat psychic.

I was always into watching TV shows and reading about ghosts and paranormal stuff. I've always kept an open mind and was fascinated by all of it. Plus in my early teen years I started realizing that I could read people much more easily than others could but I never really thought much about it.

When I told my parents I wanted to go ghost hunting to see for myself if that stuff really did exist, they thought it would be a fun activity to do with me but they didn't really believe. However, on the ghost hunt tours I could pick up on random emotions that were passing through me, or smells or sensations like hot and cold spots. Way more than everyone else would, even people who'd been doing it for a long time. So I told my parents I felt like I was a bit psychic.

My dad went along with it and my mom seemed intrigued but eventually they just sort of dismissed it, which didn't bother me since they had never experienced anything paranormal. I know it's hard to be a believer if you haven't.

So what I would like non-believers to know is that everyone is capable of becoming a bit psychic. You just need to start being open and not shut down ideas you don't understand.

***

I was 14 when I first encountered a poltergeist and throughout my life my paranormal experiences have been extensive and beyond what average investigators encounter. Since my traumatic brain injury at age 23 I have also been psychic. After 22 years of that, I now have very advanced psychic and mediumship abilities.

Recently everything has ramped up about 1,000%. I deal with my abilities every single minute of the day now. It's hard but I get through it by focusing on self-realization and teachings.

My parents always supported all my endeavors, no matter how strange, so they were very proud of me and would listen and help me work through it. They're gone now and I miss having the comfort of their physical presence.

***

I have the gifts of clairaudience and clairsentience. I hear Spirits all the time, and I am highly empathic with the living. It makes sense that I have abilities, though, because my paternal grandmother and my maternal aunt were both psychic.

There are over a thousand years of testimony and documented experiences by an incredibly wide range of people verifying that Spirits walk among us. Don't waste time ignoring the tons of information available about the Spirit world! It can really be a comfort knowing there is an amazing place awaiting us when we cease to have need for our physical bodies, and you can ease and expedite your own spiritual growth while you're still here by working with the Spirit world instead of against it.

Personally, I have had amazing paranormal experiences throughout my lifetime. The most jarring incident was being physically thrown 10-12 feet and onto my back. I was 22 years old at the time and weighed in at 205 lbs. My girlfriend was also shoved away from me with the same violent force. She was 18 so we've speculated that it might have been a poltergeist-type force that is sometimes attributed to teen girls. It freaked both of us out enough to make us go to church and read the scriptures.

I have also been touched on the head by a Spirit during a paranormal investigation. It feels like stepping into a thick spider web. I was so excited that I began hopping up and down and yelling, "Do it again, do it again!!" The other investigators looked at me like I was crazy.

I had a number of out-of-body experiences (OBE) while I was growing up, too, and I can only compare them to giving a kid LSD without explaining anything. They scared the hell out of me.

I've even had a near-death experience (NDE) in the back of an ambulance. I had just gone into ventricular fibrillation and saw a black spiraling vortex floating above me. It was frightening. I didn't have the typical "light at the end of the tunnel" deal, all I saw was black hole spiraling up into space (or so it seemed).

I cannot describe the feeling of having 800 megajoules of electricity sent through your body and into your heart but they told me (and I felt it) that I jumped a foot off the gurney. Once I was again aware of the bright lights of the ambulance, I was actually quite disturbed about not seeing any "white light" like other people talk about.

My wife is an easy one to share this stuff with, though she does worry when Spirits come to the house seeking help, which happens all the time so I make deals with them to stay away from my family if they want help from me and most have done so (with a few dramatic exceptions).

But she totally believes in Angels and has gone on several investigations with me. And she can hear the voices I play for her on my recordings once I point them out. These are called EVP's (electronic voice phenomena), and it's a talent I have that is stronger than most other people who do this work. I can pick up EVP's, I'd say 90% of which no one else can hear! And where most people can only hear a word here and there, I can hear entire conversations and distinguish multiple voices and even tell the approximate age, sex, and other unique characteristics of each individual Spirit.

I'm glad that my daughter believes, too. She can hear my recordings, like her mother. She has seen the amazing blessings that began happening after I started working with the Angels to help lost Souls cross over.

My super-intelligent son, however, refuses to believe me. He says he only hears static or noise and will not be swayed by my stories of Spirit activity. His stubborn refusal to believe what I know to be real and true does bother me sometimes. Oh well, maybe one day.

And while I've made some good friends and had a lot of fun through investigating, the most profound change in my life was also triggered by this process.

One time when reviewing my EVPs I came across the crying and pleading voice of a little boy who had died in a now covered-up well. I realized that meant he had been stuck there with his body for 100 years or so. Suddenly I was deeply distraught by the fact that this boy and countless other children I had recorded in the past were lost here in an Earth-bound state, so I contacted a psychic and sat with her as she worked with her Spirit Guide (her deceased husband) to reunite the little boy and his parents.

I have never been so moved, even to this day. I knew I had to find a way to help more Spirits because that feeling of love and satisfaction was incredible. I began attending "Soul Rescue and Spirit Release" classes a couple times a week for a few months. Since then I have helped many Spirits, as well as the families who want them out of their houses. It has been the most rewarding thing I have done in my life.

***

I see spirits sometimes, and I smell them. I had the ability as a child but lost it for a while. Then when I was in my late 20's I went into an antique mall looking for Christmas gifts and one particular store seemed to be drawing me in. As soon as I walked in I noticed how it smelled but couldn't explain it until I turned a corner and saw about 20 spirits walking around. I immediately knew that all their stuff was there so they wouldn't leave.

When I'm going through stressful times "they" send me messages through song titles or lyrics, too. For example, I was questioning a relationship that I was in and asked spirits for guidance and literally five songs in a row, the song titles were about letting go of love. Turns out he was NOT the one for me. I got my answer.

My family doesn't know about this but lots of other people do. I only tell people that I know can handle it or will "get it." Since I'm selective who I tell, I haven't had anyone be weird about it or unhelpful.

An important thing my friends do is just listen. And one friend in particular is a healer of sorts and when she was working on me she picked up right away that I have ability, so she is encouraging me to nurture it even though I'm not sure how to do that. She told me to get crystals first. Not sure what those do. I am drawn to them though.

Most people (I think) are extremely uneasy with the thought that deceased loved ones really are still around. But you have to understand that there is no heaven or hell. We all go to the same place after we die, where we continue to have lessons to learn.

Spirits need to help us in order for them to heal and grow on the other side.

***

I have always been sensitive, at an early age discovering a preference for isolation so as not to be overwhelmed by the thoughts and energetic activity of others. The exception was my younger sister, who is even more clairvoyant than I am. We connect deeply and empathically. When others observe us together, they are left scratching their heads because it's almost as though we have a secret language.

In my youth I didn't give much thought to having any special abilities, there was just a sense of being different than the community I was raised in. Being able to "know," esoterically, gave me an upper hand in my schooling, but my ability to tap into what others were feeling and thinking caused emotional turmoil as a teenager. A grounding practice would have been especially helpful back then.

As an adult, my psychic experiences occur frequently, on a daily basis, in an empathic and telepathic manner. I am highly sensitive in the areas of clairsentience and claircognizance. On rare occasion—once a year, at most—I'll see an apparition. I do not enjoy that.

The first experience that I clearly remember of an apparition came in the early days of dating my ex-husband. I left his apartment early one morning and she appeared inside my car. She was ethereal and blue and electric and looked like a hologram. I was terrified. Somehow I instantly knew her name. I fled the car and pounded on the apartment door frantically, checking over my shoulder to see if she had followed me.

When I told him her name, he turned white but assured me that I was safe and everything was fine. Then he told me who this girl had been to him and I realized that I knew about her from high school because there was a memorial on campus and teachers always talked about how special she had been. I remembered she died playing chicken with a train. But what I didn't know was that she and my ex-husband were dating at the time of her death and he had stood her up on a date that night. This information sank deep into the pit of my stomach.

She attempted to communicate with me several times in the subsequent months and I always found it terrifying. My ex-husband said she was just trying to scare me away and that she had done this to his previous girlfriends, too. Fortunately, over the next 10 years that we were together she stopped scaring me, for the most part.

Throughout my adult life I have developed my abilities through self-discovery and research, which in turn has opened doors by placing me in the path of other gifted individuals. One clairvoyant I met several years ago who is in her 60s has taken me under her wing. I consider her a guide and mentor, in addition to a dear friend. A close relationship with my acupuncturist has been crucial to my well-being, also.

I practice divination with the help of the angelic realm but I'd like to learn more about shamanism and Native American cultures and practices, too. I reinforce my strength with natural support from the bounty of the Earth plus meditation and yoga. I try to manifest my artistic gifts and gifts of service through my hair salon, my study of music and writing, and creating works of visual art.

I do not exercise my seeing ability, though, because I find it emotionally disturbing. I have clairvoyant, premonitory dreams—usually in a cluster, at least once per week, sometimes multiple times per week. I practice dream journaling, making sure to document the date and specific time, if possible.

I attempt to stay away from chemical substances that could stifle my sensitivity, but I really struggle with food. Still, it would be nice to pop a pill and numb out from the sensory bombardment, which is why I relish my time alone to help me avoid that temptation.

While I don't live in the shadows by any means, I do have to watch my tongue and tread carefully when I step beyond the threshold of my home. Sometimes, I find this amusing, as the public at large thinks they can judge books by their covers…but it's exactly that—a cover.

I do struggle with the societal stigma of psychics often being mistakenly viewed as mentally ill, though, so in a lot of ways I am still closeted. My list of confidants is really short so I have very few safe people to discuss my gifts with. And there are even different "levels of safety" with different people.

Occasionally I try to talk to my mother about these things. She listens politely but I can tell she thinks it's bullshit. She attempts to understand by asking questions but she generally discredits my accounts or dismisses them with a remark along the lines of, "Yah, you've mentioned that strange things happen to you sometimes." It makes me wonder whether the abilities that my sister and I have are genetic. Have they just skipped a generation in my mother, or perhaps she had a trauma surrounding her own abilities? I tend to lean toward the belief that psychic sensitivity is possible in everyone, some people just allow it in or choose to cultivate it while others don't. But who knows for sure?

Though I don't consider myself a Christian, I love the personal challenge in Jesus' words when he says, "Forgive them, for they know not what they do." We are all on our own paths. Some of us are following a heavy traffic pattern, some of us are blazing new trails, some of us are climbing mountains. Some of us aren't even on the ground at all. I would like for people to be open and accepting of this. Think about how "facts" are constantly changing when new research is done and new ways to observe our world are developed. It's often the heretics that end up being right when all is said and done.

***

When I was 3 years old I started seeing a man on a white horse, wearing khaki pants and a white shirt. I even asked my mom to please put a place at the table for him but she said there was no man. I cried and insisted but she did not believe me for six years, even though he continued to visit me.

Then at age 9 I was looking through some of my aunt's photo albums and started shaking violently when I saw a picture of the man on the white horse. He was riding on a beach, wearing the clothes that I always saw him in. I took the picture to my mom and told her this was the man. She turned pale and said that it was my biological father who had passed away when

I was an infant. I had no memories of him or how he looked. We didn't have any pictures around the house or anything like that.

I thought my mom didn't believe me at first. She told me later that she believed me, but was afraid for me. She explained that she had been born able to sense things and "see the future." She warned me to keep my ability secret because it would not have been accepted by my extended family, so I kept it secret for most of my life.

My mother believed me and supported me, but she did not want me to share my visions.

My husband believes me and supports me, but does not want me to share my visions.

My family preferring me to keep my visions to myself has made me secretive and insecure. But I want to tell others that it's so important to believe in yourself and your abilities. Do not be ashamed.

When I see and hear people who have passed away, they often have messages for their loved ones. For example, I have a lifelong friend whose daughter killed herself two years ago. The daughter comes to me. At first it was hard for me to tell my friend, but she accepted that I have visions of her daughter. She is supportive and believes my messages.

And I'm really lucky to have connected with a young friend who also has abilities. We often know when the other needs to talk. We share our experiences. I am free to be me around her and that is something I need very much.

ABOUT THE AUTHOR

Crystal Hope Reed has a master's degree in counseling psychology and has spent most of her professional life in the fields of counseling, mental health, and education. She's worked with clients as diverse as gifted students, domestic violence victims, the homeless, people with severe mental illnesses, and individuals and families navigating the psychic awakening process.

Since 2001, Crystal has been living her own advice about *How to Live with a Psychic.* When the full extent of Brett's psychic abilities exploded, practically overnight, she wasn't satisfied to just cope with the chaos. Instead, she tapped into her therapeutic background and intuition to figure out how people can turn this challenge into an opportunity for an even stronger relationship and an improved quality of life.

Her interest in all things metaphysical continues to grow and she will certainly be writing more books on related topics. She has also developed her own ability as a pet psychic, which she now uses to resolve issues and give animals a voice.

Crystal, Brett, and their three dogs make their home in Santa Monica, California.

If you'd like to join her mailing list, book an animal communication session, or hear more about what she has to offer, please visit her website:

www.CrystalHopeReed.com

Made in the USA
Columbia, SC
19 August 2021